MW01383599

# Lakȟótiya Wóglaka Po! - Speak Lakota!

# Level 5 Textbook

## Lakota Language Consortium

Pierre and Bloomington

i

Lakota Language Consortium is a nonprofit Lakota-led language revitalization organization.

Note: This is the student edition of the textbook. The next step in the sequence from the Lakȟótiya Wóglaka Po! - Speak Lakota! textbook series. It is designed to be used in conjunction with the Level 5 Flashcard set (ISBN 978-0-9834363-1-7) . The Level 5 Teacher's Guide is printed separately (ISBN 978-0-9834363-6-2). Please visit us at: www.lakhota.org for more information.

Lakota Language Consortium, Inc., Bloomington 47404
© 2014 by Lakota Language Consortium, Inc.
All rights reserved. Published 2014
Printed in China

19   18   17   16   15          1   2   3   4   5

ISBN-13: 978-0-9834363-0-0   (paper)

Library of Congress Control Number: 2014931259

Authors: Jan Ullrich, Kimberlee Anne Campbell, Ben Black Bear, Elizabeth Allyn Woock
Illustrations: Laura Nikiel, Elizabeth Allyn Woock
Layout: Elizabeth Allyn Woock

All rights reserved. No part of this publication may be reproduced or transmitted in any form or by any means, electronic or mechanical, including photocopy, recording, or any information storage and retrieval system, without permission in writing from the publisher.

Visit us at: **www.lakhota.org**

# ACKNOWLEDGMENTS

This textbook was made possible through the contributions of over 50 language consultants and advisors from across the region.

We are thankful to: Dewey Bad Warrior, Ben Black Bear, Sandra Black Bear, Richard Black Elk, Gabe Black Moon, Florida Bull Bear-Jealous, Helene Circle Eagle, Marilyn Circle Eagle, Iris Eagle Chasing, Gladys Hawk, Paulette High Elk, Suela High Elk, Manny Iron Hawk, Philomine Lakota, Darlene Last Horse, Shirley Lefthand, Bernadine Little Thunder, Ken Little Thunder, Elisabeth Makes Him First, Helmina Makes Him First, Lyle Noisy Hawk Sr., Darlene Red Bear, Tom Red Bird, Mary Ann Red Cloud, Dainna Red Owl, Verola Spider, Edward Starr, Delores Taken Alive, Ray Takes War Bonnet, and Robert Two Crow.

There have been friends and supporters whose indirect help was critical to making this Textbook achieve publication: the LLC Board of Directors, the Cheyenne River Sioux Tribe, the members of the lakotadictionary.org Forum, and the many Lakota language activists around Lakota country.

Images of Lakota persons on page 18 are published with the kind permission of Billy Mills, Kevin Locke, Jodi Archambault Gillette, family of Clarence Wolf Guts, Arvol Looking Horse, World Wisdom Publishing, the South Dakota Historical Society, Joseph Marshall III, and Arthur Amiotte. Thanks also to Stars and Stripes, the Bush Foundation and the White House Office of Media Affairs for their assistance.

The Level 5 Textbook was made possible through the generous financial contributions of: Administration for Native Americans, Native Language Preservation and Maintenance Category - Native Language Project Implementation Grant No: 90NL0489, the Michael T. Riordan Family Foundation, The FHL Foundation the Tatanka Oyate Verein of Germany, the Moore Charitable Trust, and the Lakota Herbs/ HPI Health Products, Inc. **Wóphila Thánkal**

# Table of Contents

# Table of Contents

# Introduction

## For Students

You've come a long way! There are lots of new words to learn in Lakota this year. Come with us! Let's have fun learning!

## For Teachers

Your students can say a lot of sentences in Lakota now! But they need to go further. It is up to you to get the students to talk in Lakota as much as possible during class time. This is your opportunity to push them to expand their horizons and talk about different things. Use this book and the teachers' guide to prepare for each activity and to contextualize the language. You can make each lesson come alive.

## For Independent Learners

You're now ready for Level 5! As you progress, sometimes you may feel frustrated. Every language learner feels this way sometimes. One of the most important things to remember is to make learning Lakota a part of your everyday life. Make a special time for yourself to learn something every day. Spending 15 minutes with Lakota daily will move you forward faster than cramming your effort into one day a week. You will see the results by the time you have finished the book.

## For Parents and others who are supporting learners through the journey toward Lakota fluency

When your child or someone you care about is learning Lakota, they need your support! Show your interest in what they can say and write in Lakota. As a a parent or grandparent we need to also help them find time and space to study.

The Lakota language teacher needs your support too! It is important to be positive about the vocabulary words and sentences in the lessons. It is easy to be critical, but both students and teachers need all the support you can give them; even if they are teaching words you don't use every day. Students are sometimes introduced to words from other communities or to less common words. These variations make the language rich.

**Here are some Lakota values that will help you in your quest to learn Lakota:**

### Wóohitike – Courage

Be courageous in the challenging quest of learning Lakota. Be brave enough to learn new words, sentence patterns and Lakota thinking. Your courage will be an example for other language students.

### Wówauŋšila – Compassion

Have compassion for others on this learning quest. Be compassionate with the errors of others and help them learn.

### Wówačhaŋtognake – Generosity

Be generous in sharing whatever you have learned with others. Speak with them in Lakota every chance you get and where ever you can.

### Wóksape – Wisdom

Gain wisdom by learning to love learning. Understand that no one knows everything about the language, and that we can all learn from each other. Your wisdom can compare various teaching materials and evaluate their quality.

### Wówačhiŋtȟaŋka - Patience, Perseverance, Self-discipline

Patience and self-discipline help you persevere in learning. Never give up, strive in spite of obstacles and difficulties. In your daily schedule set aside at least two 15-20 minute slots for learning every day. Set a goal of how many words and sentences you are going to learn every week.

### Wóyuonihaŋ – Respect

Show respect for the ancestral language by learning the correct pronunciation, spelling and sentence patterns. Value your language by respecting these standards; they maintain the authenticity and uniqueness of the language and culture. Show respect to anyone who learns Lakota regardless of who they are.

### Wóuŋšiič'iye – Humility

Be humble about your knowledge and make your learning a life-changing spiritual quest. Don't brag about your achievements and don't use the language in destructive ways or for self-serving purposes.

**1** Lisa and Bob are looking around in Lisa's grandma's shed to see what's in there! Why don't you help them? Take a look around the shed! Do you know the names of those things in Lakota? On a piece of scrap paper, make a list of all things you see that you can say in Lakota.

**2** Skim through part of the dialogue that is on this page, and answer the question below.

Lisa táku čha iyéya he?

a) **Wóžuha waŋží iyéye.**    b) **Čháŋthipi waŋží iyéye.**    č) **Takúku óta iyéye.**

**Má lé! Uŋčí tȟa-čháŋthipi kiŋ mahél wóžuha waŋ iyéwaye. Paŋȟyá oówaŋyaŋg wašté kštó.**

**Huŋhuŋhé! Uŋgná sáŋm óta mahél yaŋké. Éwaŋuŋyaŋka héči!**

**Lél wóžuha k'uŋ hé iyéwaye kštó.**

**Oháŋ, isáŋm waúŋkole kte. Uŋgnáš takúŋl isáŋm iyéuŋyiŋ kte séče.**

**3** Now look through the dialogue on the next page. Did Bob and Lisa find the same things that you did? What items did they find in the shed? Make a list on a piece of scrap paper.

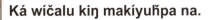

Ká wíčalu kiŋ makíyuȟpa na.

Oháŋ, iyówahi háŋtaŋš čhičíyuȟpiŋ kte.

Ká míyožuha kiŋ imákiču yetȟó.

Oháŋ! Líla oówaŋyaŋg wašté kštó.

Ká maswógnaka tȟáŋka kiŋ íŋš tók? Hiyúmakhiya na! Uŋgnáš owíŋla etáŋ él úŋ séče.

Oháŋ, hiyúčhičhiyiŋ kte.

Hoští, maswógnaka kiŋ él tágni úŋ šni.

Oháŋ, héktakiya éwagnakiŋ kte.

Wóžuha kiŋ hená íŋš tók? Makípahi na hiyúmakhiyiŋ yetȟó.

Tuwá lé! Líla škaŋyákapiŋ kštó. Oháŋ, čhičípahi kte.

Wáŋ, lé šiyótȟaŋka waŋ! Bluȟá owákihi he?

Tókša uŋčí imúŋǧiŋ kte.

Lé čhaŋóphiye kiŋ oyúǧaŋ šíče! Makíyuǧaŋ na!

Tókhe líla húŋkešni yélakȟa! Haha. Ho čha, wáŋčag čhičíyuǧaŋ kte.

Wáŋ lé haŋp'íkčeka waštéšte!

Makípazo na. Háŋ, líla waštéšte.

Wáŋ k'éya! Lisa tȟaŋíŋ šni áye.

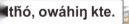

Itȟó, owáhiŋ kte.

Lisa tókhi iyáya hwo?

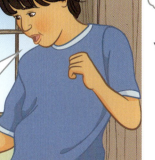

Lisa, tókhi ilála hwo? Uŋgnáhelaka waŋčhíyaŋke šni. Lisa tókȟaȟ'aŋ.

**4** Now read the dialogue on page 3 again. Who did each activity? Who did they do it for? Can you figure it out? Write the correct name in each blank.

a) _____Bob_____  _____Lisa_____  wíčalu kiŋ hé kiyúȟpe.

b) _____  _____  míyožuha kiŋ hé ikíču.

č) _____  _____  maswógnaka tȟáŋka kiŋ hé hiyúkhiye.

e) _____  _____  wóžuha kiŋ hená kipáhi.

g) _____  _____  čhaŋóphiye kiŋ hé kiyúǧaŋ.

ǧ) _____  _____  haŋp'íkčeka kiŋ kipázo.

**5** Can you answer these questions about what Bob and Lisa were doing in Grandma's cabin? Look back at the dialogue again if you need some help.

a) Táku čha tȟokéya waŋyáŋkapi he?  _____

b) Tuwá maswógnaka tȟáŋka kiŋ waŋyáŋka he?  _____

č) Tuwá wóžuha kiŋ hená pahí he?  _____

e) Tuwá čhaŋóphiye kiŋ yuǧáŋ he?  _____

g) Čhaŋóphiye kiŋ hetáŋhaŋ táku čha ičúpi he?  _____

ǧ) Maswógnaka tȟáŋka kiŋ mahél táku čha iyéyapi he?  _____

**6** Now it's your turn to help your friends out! Pretend you are at a friend's garden/storage shed, getting ready for a camping trip. When your friend asks, take down the item he /she asks for.

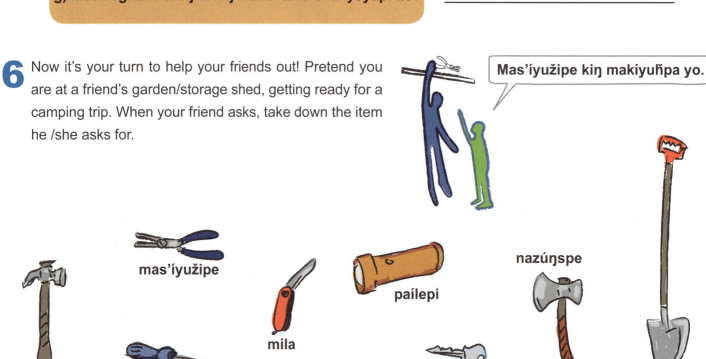

Mas'íyužipe kiŋ makíyuȟpa yo.

mas'íyužipe

nazúŋspe

paílepi

míla

mas'íyapȟe

wíyuhomni

iyúšloke

makhínapte

**7** Now talk to three different people in the class. Each one will have something that a classmate got down for them. Ask them who got it down for them, like the model.

Tuwé čha _____ kiŋ lé ničíyuȟpa he?

David _____ kiŋ lé makíyuȟpe.

**8** Then, write some sentences about what happened at the storage locker, like the models.

Peter Betty wíčazo kiŋ kiyúȟpe.

_____

_____

_____

_____

_____

**9** Now let's try something else. Stand in a circle. Your teacher will give each of you a picture of something. Hold it up so everyone else can see it! Now, ask one of your classmates to pass you what he/she has, like the model:

(Wówapi) kiŋ hiyúmakhiya yo/ye.

**10** Now, write sentences about the things that were handed to you, like the model:

(David) (wówapi) kiŋ hiyúmakhiye.

_____

_____

_____

**11** What did they pass to one another? Write sentences about your classmates, like the model:

(Susie) (John) (wówapi) kiŋ hiyúkhiye.

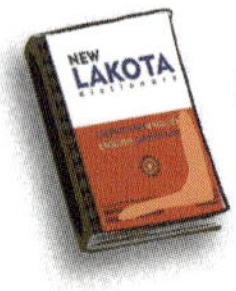

**12** **a** How do we figure out where personal affixes (me, you, I, etc.) go in a verb? If we know where the "I" form goes, then we know where to put everything else! (Remember, except for "we," which often goes in a different spot.) Let's look at the dictionary! **Find the "I" form for each of the verbs and write it in the blank.**

**kiyúȟpA**

**ikíču**

**hiyúkhiyA**

**kiyúšičA**

**kipáhi**

**kiyúǧaŋ**

kiyúha [LYS] (ki- yuhá) V-DAT to have or keep smth for sb or towards sb. • Wíŋyaŋ kiŋ lé iyúha wówahečhuŋ uŋkíyuhapi. We all have some relation to this woman. Wówauŋšila mayákiluha. You had kindness for me. Wóanawizi makíyuha. He holds jealousy towards me ▶ 1s: wakíyuha / wakíbluha. 2s: yakíyuha / yakíluha. 1p: uŋkíyuhapi.

◇ kiyúȟla [L] (ki- yuȟlá) V-DAT to give sb a phone call. Lit. 'to ring another's.' Usage: this is in fact a three valence slot verb, but one of the arguments (phone) is always underlying. • Makíyuȟla yo. Give me a call. Čhičíyuȟla kte. I will give you a call. Mayákiluȟla he? Did you call me? ▶ 1s: wakíyuȟla / wakíbluȟla. 2s: yakíyuȟla / yakíluȟla. 1p: uŋkíyuȟlapi. ○ Y.S.: kiyúȟda.

kiyúȟpA [LYS] (ki- yuȟpÁ) V-DAT to unload smth for sb; to

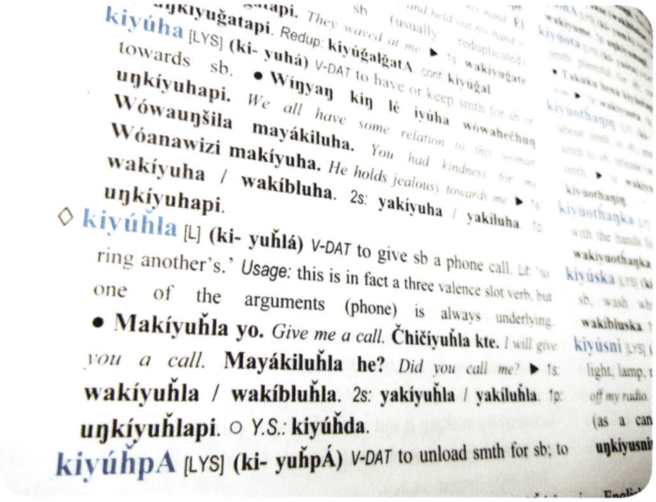

**b** In verbs that include "**ki**" or "**khi**," where do the personal affixes go? Circle the correct answer.

a. Before "**ki**" or "**khi**". b. After "**ki**" or "**khi**". c. At the beginning of the word.

**č** Can you add "me" (**ma**) to each of the verbs below? Hint: each of these verbs has "**ki**" or "**khi**"!

| | | | |
|---|---|---|---|
| **kiyúȟpA** | | **kiyúšičA** | |
| **ikíču** | | **kipáhi** | |
| **hiyúkhiyA** | | **kiyúǧaŋ** | |
| **kiúŋ** | | **ekíyA** | |

**13** Pick one of your classmates, and give them a command using one of these verbs, like the model: **kiyúȟpA, ikíču, hiyúkhiyA, kipáhi, kiyúǧaŋ.** Your partner will do what you have told them to do. Then, tell the teacher what your partner did for you.

David, wówapi kiŋ makípahi na/yetȟó.

David wówapi kiŋ makípahi.

**14** Let's review how to say that "I" do something to or for "you." Remember, when we have a "k," we also need to make some changes in spelling.
**Look at the model, and then change the other verbs to say that "I" did it for "you."**

kiyúȟpA $\longrightarrow$ čhičíyuȟpe

ikíču $\longrightarrow$ _____

mas'ákipȟA $\longrightarrow$ _____

hiyúkhiyA $\longrightarrow$ _____

kiyúšičA $\longrightarrow$ _____

kipáhi $\longrightarrow$ _____

kiyútA $\longrightarrow$ _____

kiyúǧaŋ $\longrightarrow$ _____

tȟebkhíyA $\longrightarrow$ _____

kiúŋ $\longrightarrow$ _____

ekíyA $\longrightarrow$ _____

**15** **a**  Now let's look at these 5 verbs again: **kiyúŋpA, ikíču, hiyúkhiyA, kipáhi, kiyúǧaŋ.** Stand in a circle with your classmates. First, the teacher will give each one of you a flashcard or object. You decide what to do with it: You can hold it, put it on the ground, or tape it up to the wall.

**b**  Next, choose one of your classmates. Look at where they have put their object or flashcard. Using one of the 5 verbs, ask them to do something for you, like the model. This time, your partner should answer talking about what he/she will do for you, like the model.

**Wówapi kiŋ hiyúmakhiya yo!**

**Oháŋ, wówapi kiŋ hiyúčhičhiyiŋ kte!**

**č**  After you have listened to everybody, write four or five sentences about what your classmates did for each other. Follow the model:

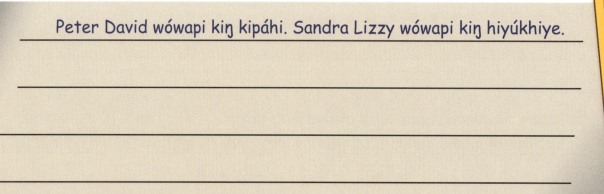

Peter David wówapi kiŋ kipáhi. Sandra Lizzy wówapi kiŋ hiyúkhiye.

**16**  You are getting thirsty! On the table, there are pictures of several things to drink. Choose a drink you would like, and ask a classmate to take the drink for you. Then, ask your classmate to open it for you, like the model:

**(Asáŋpi) waŋží imákiču we.**

**Oháŋ, (asáŋpi) waŋží ičhíčiču kte!**

**(Asáŋpi) kiŋ lé makíyuǧaŋ yo!**

**Oháŋ, (asáŋpi) kiŋ hé čhičíyuǧaŋ kte.**

**17** **a** Now, write three pairs of sentences about what your classmates did for each other, like the model. Two of the pairs should be TRUE (something that really happened in exercise 16). One of the pairs should be FALSE (it didn't happen).

(Sarah) (John) (asáŋpi) waŋ ikíču.  (Sarah)(John) (asáŋpi) kiŋ kiyúǧaŋ.

_____

_____

_____

**b** Next, read your sentences to a partner. Can s/he pick out the false sentences? Try this with 2 other partners! How many of them got it right?

**18** **a** What if someone took your drink on you? Sit in a circle, with your eyes closed and the card with your drink on it in front of you. Your teacher will choose one of you to be the mischief maker!  What will you say if your drink is gone when you open your eyes?  Look at the models!

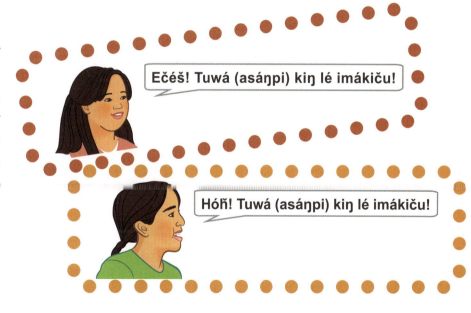

Ečéš! Tuwá (asáŋpi) kiŋ lé imákiču!

Hóȟ! Tuwá (asáŋpi) kiŋ lé imákiču!

**b** Write 2 sentences about what just happened to your classmates, like the model:
Tuwá (Serene) (asáŋpi) kiŋ ikíču.

_____

_____

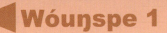 

**19** The childrens' cousins are visiting, but they're little kids! Sometimes, they spill things, or break them on the children! Look at the verbs below, and then finish the speech bubbles for each of the children.

kiyúsotA

kipápsuŋ

šabkhíyA

kiyúweǧA

kíčala

Susie mázaska makíyusote!

Peter

Debbie

Brandon

Shantay

Lisa tókhi iyáya hwo?

Tókhel ilúkčaŋ hwo?

**20** So what do you think happened to Lisa? Read the coyote's question, and circle the best answer.

Lisa tȟaŋkátakiya máni kéčhaŋmi.

Lisa uŋgnáhela tókȟaȟ'aŋ kéčhaŋmi.

Lisa čhaŋóphiye kiŋ akáŋl íyotaka kéčhaŋmi.

**1** Skim through the dialogue below, and circle the best answer.

Waŋná Lisa tuktél nážiŋ hwo?

a) Mnilúzahe Otȟúŋwahe-ta nážiŋ.
b) Pahá waŋ akáŋl nážiŋ.
č) Obláye waŋ él nážiŋ.
e) Ȟé waŋ akáŋl nážiŋ.
g) Čháŋ waŋ oȟláthe nážiŋ.

| | |
|---|---|
| Lisa: | **Tuktél waúŋ he? Tomákča he?** |
| Tȟaté Wiŋ: | Nitúwe he? Tuktétaŋhaŋ yahí he? |
| Lisa: | **Tókhe, Lakȟótiyaye so? Lisa emáčiyapi. Níš táku eníčiyapi he?** |
| TW: | Tȟaté-wiŋ emáčiyapi. Tuktétaŋhaŋ yahí he? |
| Lisa: | **Uŋčí tȟa-čháŋthipi kiŋ mahél nawážiŋ na heháŋl haŋp'íkčeka kiŋ lená owáhe. Yuŋkȟáŋ tókȟamaȟ'aŋ.** |
| TW: | Hayápi eyá núŋ kiŋ hená táku he? Líla tȟogyé niglúze. |
| Lisa: | **Hayápi nitȟáwa kiŋ oówaŋyaŋg waštéšte. Hená tuwá níčaǧa he?** |
| TW: | Iná míčaǧe. Loyáčhiŋ he? Loyáčhiŋ héči wičhóthi-ta uŋgníŋ kte. |
| Lisa: | **Háŋ, lowáčhiŋ. Tuktél yathí he? Letáŋhaŋ toháŋyaŋ yathí he?** |
| TW: | Tȟéhaŋtu šni. Pahá kiŋ hé akȟótaŋhaŋ uŋthípi. Hó we, uŋyíŋ kte. |

**2** Now, read through the dialogue again, and circle the best answer to each question.

**1** Lisa tuwá waŋyáŋka he?
a) Lakȟóta wičháša waŋ waŋyáŋke.
č) Lakȟóta wičhíŋčala waŋ waŋyáŋke.
b) Wašíču wičhíŋčala waŋ waŋyáŋke.

**2** Wičhíŋčala waŋ Lisa atáye kiŋ táku iyá he?
a) Lakȟól'iye.
b) Šahíyela iyé.
č) Wašíču iyé.

**3** Lakȟóta wičhíŋčala kiŋ hé táku ečíyapi he?
a) Pȟehíŋ Žiží-wiŋ
č) Tȟaté-wiŋ
b) Tȟašúŋke Óta-wiŋ

**4** Lisa haŋp'íkčeka kiŋ ohán yuŋkȟáŋ obláye waŋ él hinážiŋ. Tákuwe?
a) Ičhíŋ haŋp'íkčeka kiŋ tȟaŋnígnila čha hé uŋ.
b) Ičhíŋ haŋp'íkčeka kiŋ wakȟáŋ čha hé uŋ.
č) Ičhíŋ haŋp'íkčeka kiŋ kȟúŋšitku tȟáwa čha hé uŋ.

**5** Lisa hayápi tȟáwa kiŋ étkiya Tȟaté-wiŋ tókhel tȟawáčhiŋ he?
a) Lisa tȟa-háyapi kiŋ líla oówaŋyaŋg waštéšte kéčhiŋ.
b) Lisa tȟa-háyapi kiŋ líla šabšápe kéčhiŋ.
č) Lisa tȟa-háyapi kiŋ líla oštéštekiŋ na tȟoktȟókča kéčhiŋ.

**6** Tȟaté-wiŋ tȟa-háyapi kiŋ tuwá kíčaǧa hwo?
a) Kȟúŋšitku kiŋ hayápi kiŋ kíčaǧe.
b) Tȟuŋwíŋču kiŋ hayápi kiŋ kíčaǧe.
č) Húŋku kiŋ hayápi kiŋ kíčaǧe.

**7** Lisa Tȟaté-wiŋ kičhí tókhiya yápi he?
a) Wayáwa yápi.
b) Wičhóthi-ta yápi.
č) Mas'óphiye-ta yápi.

**8** Lisa tóktuka he?
a) Lisa líla ípuze.
b) Lisa líla ȟwá.
č) Lisa líla ločhíŋ.

**3** We know Lisa met Tȟaté Wiŋ out on the plains, but **when** did Tȟaté Wiŋ live? Look up the words below in the dictionary. Draw lines to match the words in the left-hand column to the words or dates that fit best on the right.

Then circle the date that is the most likely date for the meeting between Tȟaté Wiŋ and Lisa.

| | |
|---|---|
| eháŋk'ehaŋ | 4030 |
| lečhálake s'e | 2011 |
| leháŋl | waŋná |
| tȟokátakiya | 1857 |

**4** # Abléza po!

**a** In English many question words begin with **wh**, as in **wh**ere, **wh**en, **wh**o, **wh**y, **wh**at, **wh**ich. What letter do most Lakota question words begin with? Look at the sample questions below to find out.

Write it here: _____

**b** Now, match the questions on the left with the English sentence that is most similar on the right.

| | |
|---|---|
| Tuwá hí he? | How are you? |
| Hé tuwé he? | Where do you live? |
| Táku luhá he? | What do you have? |
| Tókhiya lá he? | Why did you do it? |
| Tuktél yathí he? | What is going on? |
| Tóhaŋ yaglí he? | Who is she? |
| Toháŋl yaú kta he? | Where are you going? |
| Tóna luhá he? | How many do you have? |
| Tókhel yaúŋ he? | What is it like? |
| Tákuwe ečhánuŋ he? | Who came? |
| Tókȟa he? | When did you come back? |
| Tókča he? (Tókheča he?) | When will you come? |

Huŋhuŋhé! Wičhóiye kiŋ lená óta. Ho po, húŋȟ uŋspéuŋkič'ičhiyapi kte.

**5** Let's take a survey! Talk to three different classmates. Ask all of the questions to each person, and take notes on the answers.

| | | | |
|---|---|---|---|
| Táku eníčiyapi he? | | | |
| Tuktél yathí he? | | | |
| Tóhaŋ nitȟúŋpi he? | | | |
| Nihúŋ táku ečíyapi he? | | | |
| Táku wóyute waštéyalaka he? | | | |
| Waníyaŋpi tóna wičháluha he? | | | |

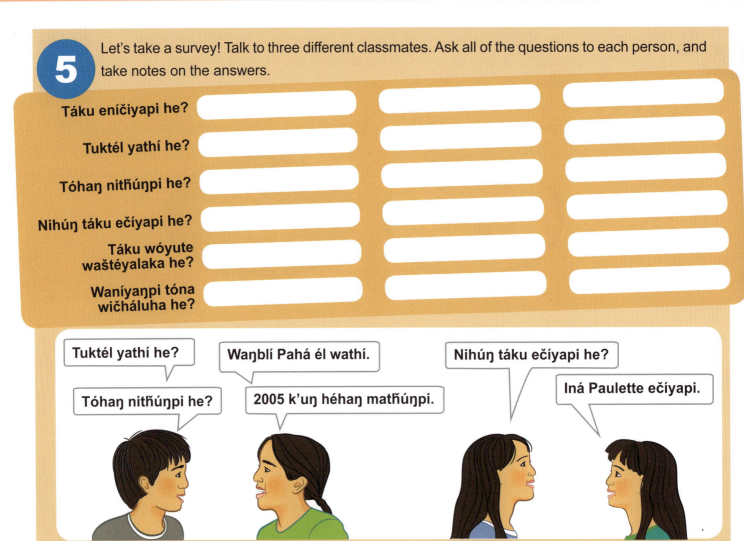

> Tuktél yathí he?

> Waŋblí Pahá él wathí.

> Nihúŋ táku ečíyapi he?

> Tóhaŋ nitȟúŋpi he?

> 2005 k'uŋ héhaŋ matȟúŋpi.

> Iná Paulette ečíyapi.

**6** **Abléza po!**

There are two ways to ask about "where" in Lakota: **Tuktél** and **Tókhiya**. Read the four sentences below and then answer these questions:

Which one of these words asks about "moving in a direction, where to"?
Write it here: _____

Which one of these words talks about "at what place," or "where without any movement"?
Write it here: _____

**Bob tuktél nážiŋ he?**

**David tókhiya íŋyaŋka he?**

**Lisa tuktél thí he?**

**Jamie tókhiya yá he?**

**7** Can you add the correct question word to these sentences? Decide whether you should use "**tuktél**" or "**tókhiya**" in each case, and write the word in the blank.

1. Peter _____ yaŋká he?

2. Joe _____ tȟúŋpi he?

3. Kimi _____ yíŋ kta he?

4. Bob blokétu k'uŋ héhaŋ _____ í he?

5. Tom _____ yá he?

6. Tȟašína _____ iyáya he?

7. Matȟó _____ wayáwa he?

8. Kiŋyékhiyapi kiŋ _____ kiŋyáŋ he?

vbv10. Ptéȟčaka kiŋ _____ wayášlapi he?

11. Igmú kiŋ _____ ištíŋma he?

**8** Let's make a survey that you can give some of your classmates. Ask three classmates each of the questions, and fill in the chart with their answers. Some possible answers are listed, but you can make up your own answers too!

**a** Tuktél nitȟúŋpi he?

Mike — Mnilúzahe Otȟúŋwahe él matȟúŋpi.

**b** Waníyetu nizáptaŋ k'uŋ héhaŋ tuktél yathí he?

Mike — Waníyetu mazáptaŋ k'uŋ héhaŋ Wazí Aháŋhaŋ él wathí.

**č** Híŋhaŋni kiŋháŋ tókhiya níŋ kta he?

Mike — Owáyawa-ta mníŋ kte.

**e** Aŋpétu waŋží él tókhiya níŋ kte ȟčiŋ he?

Mike — Pȟečhókaŋ Háŋska Makȟóčhe él mníŋ kte ȟčíŋ.

**9** Can you figure out who your partner is thinking about? Ask your partner questions, like the model conversations, and see if you can guess the right name! Be careful to use the correct question word, **tuktél** or **tókhiya**. If you guess correctly, color the picture in!

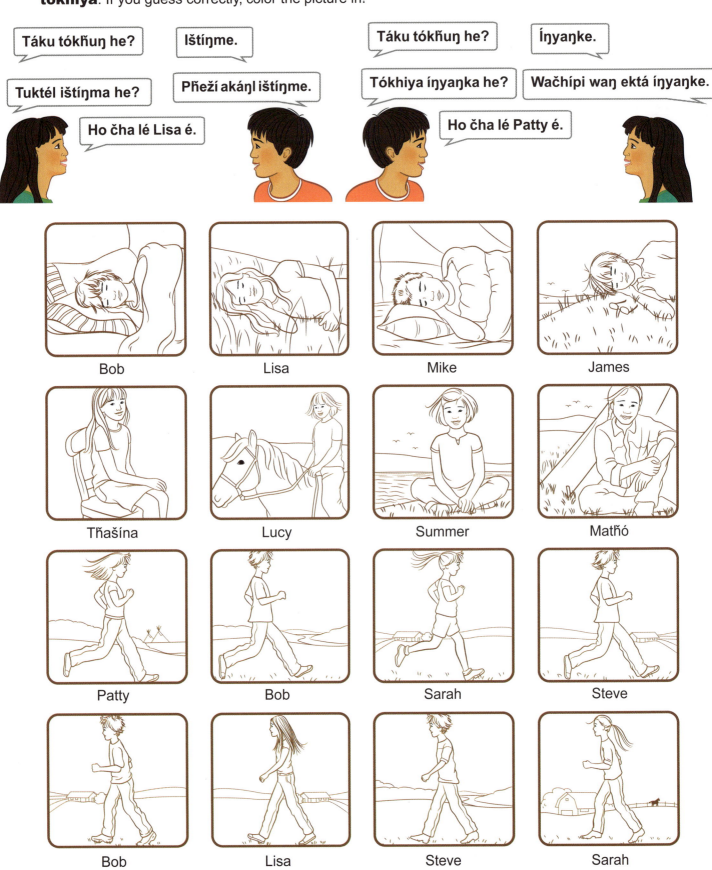

## 10  Abléza po!

Who did it? Who is it? Lakota has two words to ask "who". They are **tuwá** and **tuwé**.

One of them is always followed by a verb. Look at the sentences below and figure out which one it is.

Write the word here: _____

Tuwá hí he?                    Hokšíla kiŋ hé tuwé he?

Tuwá waŋláka he?               Wičhíŋčala kiŋ hé tuwé he?

Tuwá ečhúŋ he?                 Wičháša kiŋ hé tuwé he?

Tuwá aténiyaŋ he?             Hé tuwé he?

## 11

Now it's your turn! Fill in the blanks with the correct word - **tuwá** or **tuwé**.

a) Haŋp'íkčeka kiŋ  _____  káǧa he?

b) Hokšíla háŋske kiŋ hé _____ he?

č) Iyéčhiŋkyaŋke kiŋ ilázata _____ nážiŋ he?

e) _____  waŋyáŋg yaí he?

g) _____  óničiya he?

ǧ) Wičháša waŋ wapȟáha waŋ úŋ kiŋ hé _____ he?

h) Tȟaspáŋ kiŋ  _____  ičú he?

ȟ) Ni _____  he?

## 12

Who is doing what activity? Your teacher will give you an activity card. Then, go around the room. Each of you will ask a question, like the model. The person doing the activity will answer. Try to remember who is doing which activity! When you sit down, write as many sentences about what you heard as you can!

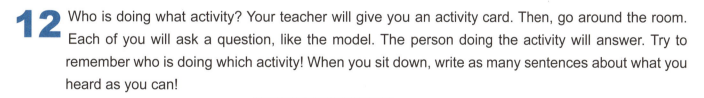

Tuwá íŋyaŋka he?

Miyé čha waíŋmnaŋke.

**13** Look at these pictures of well-known Lakota and Dakota people. First, try to match the pictures with the written descriptions. Then, with your partner, take turns asking who each person is, and identifying them, like the model. After that, if you are not sure about some of the people, ask the teacher.

1. **Clarence Wolf Guts** – Okíčhize Tȟáŋka Ičínuŋpa él naȟmála ikȟáŋčhola uŋ Lakȟól'iya wóglake.

2. **Ptesáŋ Wiŋ** – Ptehíŋčala Čhaŋnúŋpa kiŋ Lakȟóta oyáte kiŋ líla eháŋni wičhákahi.

3. **Billy Mills** – 1964 k'uŋ héhaŋ Olympic Akíčhiyapi ektá khiíŋyaŋkapi kiŋ ohíye.

4. **Joseph Marshal III.** – Eháŋni Lakȟóta wičhóuŋ kiŋ ečhétkiya wówapi káǧe s'a.

5. **Kevin Locke** – Lakȟól wačhí wičháša waŋ makȟásitomniyaŋ očháštȟuŋke.

6. **Ziŋtkála Šá (Gertrude Simmons Bonnin)** – Lakȟóta wičhóoyake óta owá.

7. **Arvol Looking Horse** – Ptehíŋčala Čhaŋnúŋpa wakȟáŋ kiŋ awáŋyaŋke.

8. **Ella Deloria** – Lakȟól wičhóȟ'aŋ na Lakȟól'iyapi kiŋ pasí na owá égnake.

9. **Jodi Gillette** – Thi-ská kiŋ ektá Tȟuŋkášilayapi kiŋ ókiye.

10. **Tȟatȟáŋka Íyotake** – Húŋkpapȟa kiŋ itȟáŋčhaŋyaŋpi.

11. **Arthur Amiotte** – Líla yupȟíya itówapi káǧe.

12. **Maȟpíya Lúta** – Oglála kiŋ itȟáŋčhaŋyaŋpi.

Lé tuwé he?
Lé Kevin Locke é.

**14** Now let's see what you remember! With a partner, take turns asking and answering the questions about the activities of the people on page 18. Write your answers in the blanks.

1. Tuwá okíčhize él ikȟáŋčhola ogná wóglaka he?

_____

2. Tuwá Ptehíŋčala Čhaŋnúŋpa Wakȟáŋ kiŋ Lakȟóta kiŋ wičhákahi he?

_____

3. Tuwá Thi-ská ektá wówaši ečhúŋ he?

_____

4. Tuwá Olympic khiíŋyaŋkapi waŋ ohíya he?

_____

5. Tuwá Lakȟól wačhí he?

_____

6. Tuwá Lakȟóta wičhóȟ'aŋ na Lakȟól'iyapi pasí khuwá he?

_____

_____

7. Tuwá líla yuphíya itówapi káǧa he?

_____

8. Eháŋni Oglála kiŋ tuwá itȟáŋčhaŋyaŋpi he?

_____

9. Eháŋni Húŋkpapȟa kiŋ tuwá itȟáŋčhaŋyaŋpi he?

_____

**15** Read what the coyote is thinking about what is happening to Lisa now, and select the best answer to each of his questions by circling the correct picture.

Lisa Tȟaté-wiŋ kičhí Lakȟóta wičhóthi-ta iyáyapi.
Hél táku čha waŋyáŋka hwo?

**a** Eháŋni Lakȟóta oyáte kiŋ iyéčhiŋkiŋyaŋke óta yuhápi naíŋš šúŋkawakȟáŋ óta wičháyuhapi hwo?

**b** Iǧúǧa očhéthi naíŋš mas'óčhethi uŋ lol'íȟ'aŋpi hwo?

**č** Mní naíŋš mnikápȟopapi yatkáŋpi hwo?

**e** Lisa táku čha yútiŋ kta hwo? Ptéȟčaka tȟaló naíŋš omníča yužápi?

**1** Look at what the coyote is saying about what Lisa is doing. Where is she standing with Tȟaté-wiŋ? Circle the correct picture.

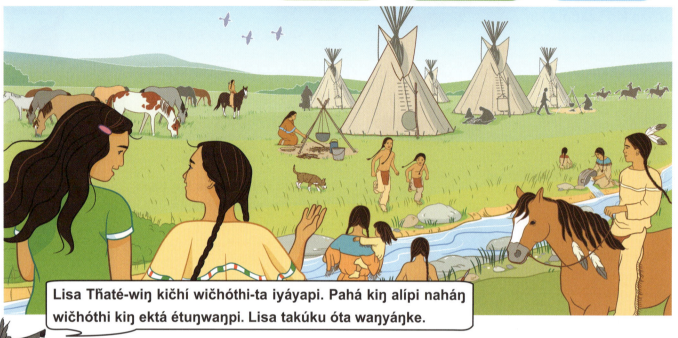

Lisa Tȟaté-wiŋ kičhí wičhóthi-ta iyáyapi. Pahá kiŋ alípi naháŋ wičhóthi kiŋ ektá étuŋwaŋpi. Lisa takúku óta waŋyáŋke.

**2** What are the girls looking at?
Circle the correct picture.

**3** Can you find the word meaning "to climb up, to climb over"? Hint: you can find it by remembering where the girls are standing! Write the word here: _____

**4** **a** Take a look at the picture on pages 22 and 23. Can you make a list of things you see that you know how to say in Lakota?

1. _____   5. _____   9. _____

2. _____   6. _____   10. _____

3. _____   7. _____

4. _____   8. _____

**b** Now, compare your list with two other students in your class. What did they put on their lists that you didn't have?

**5** Look at the picture on pages 22 and 23 again. Write down 3 words for things you see that you don't remember or don't know how to say in Lakota. Then, find the Lakota word for the item in the dictionary.

Uŋgnáš wičhóiye kiŋ lená húŋȟ yéksuye šni séče. Wičhóiye wówapi kiŋ úŋ po. Wičhóiye kiŋ hená olé po.

_____  _____

_____  _____

_____  _____

**6** Lisa is listening to many of the people at Tȟaté Wiŋ's village. They are explaining to her what they are doing. She wants to make some notes so she remembers everything! Can you help her? Rewrite what each person says from the "I" form to the "he/she" form.

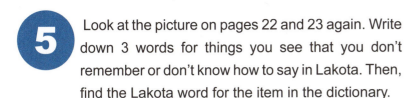

čhuwíč'iŋpa waŋ wéč'iŋ ⟶ *čhuwíč'iŋpa waŋ kič'íŋ*

**Wákhil nawážiŋ.** _____

**Šiyótȟaŋka waŋ blažó.** _____

**Pápa eyá puswáye.** _____

**Ptehíŋšma waŋ kpaŋwáye.** _____

**Čhaŋwák'iŋ.** _____

**Šúŋkawakȟáŋ waŋ wíwayuŋ.** _____

**Wawákaǧeǧe.** _____

**Tȟaló wakábla.** _____

**Čhéǧa waŋ blužáža.** _____

**Waníyetu iyáwapi waŋ wakáǧe.** _____

**Tȟaló wapásnuŋ.** _____

**Čhaŋwákabu.** _____

## 7 Abléza po!

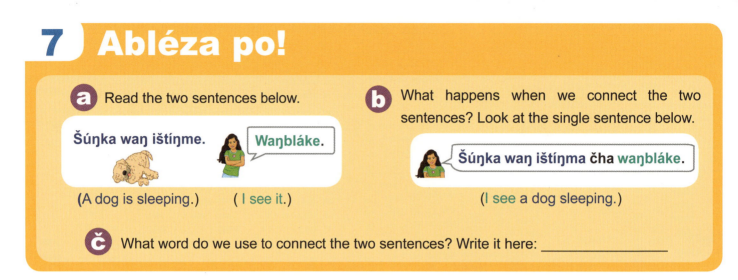

**a** Read the two sentences below.

Šúŋka waŋ ištíŋme. Waŋbláke.

(A dog is sleeping.) ( I see it.)

**b** What happens when we connect the two sentences? Look at the single sentence below.

Šúŋka waŋ ištíŋma čha waŋbláke.

(I see a dog sleeping.)

**č** What word do we use to connect the two sentences? Write it here: _____

**8** Lisa is talking about what she sees. But, she might try to trick you! Are all of the sentences below true about the picture on pages 22 and 23? Circle the sentences that are true. Cross out the sentences that are false.

Wíŋyaŋ waŋ čhaŋk'íŋ čha waŋbláke.

Wakȟáŋheža waŋ čhéya čha waŋbláke.

Winúȟčala waŋ wakáǧeǧe yaŋká čha waŋbláke.

Maštíŋčala waŋ psíča čha waŋbláke.

Wičhíŋčala waŋ lowáŋ čha waŋbláke.

Wičháša waŋ wákhil nážiŋ čha waŋbláke.

Wičháša waŋ mni-yátkaŋ čha waŋbláke.

Šúŋkawakȟáŋ waŋ máni čha waŋbláke.

Šúŋkawakȟáŋ waŋ íŋyaŋka čha waŋbláke.

Šúŋkawakȟáŋ waŋ mni-yátkaŋ čha waŋbláke.

Wíŋyaŋ waŋ nuŋwáŋ čha waŋbláke.

Hokšíla waŋ nuŋwáŋ čha waŋbláke.

**9 a** Lisa looks at the camp and says "I see a dog sleeping." How about you? What do you see a dog doing? Look at the picture and finish writing the four sentences about what you see, like Lisa's model. Be careful! You won't use all the words listed below. Cross out the ones that are not in the camp picture.

wapȟápȟa     ikpáptaŋptaŋ     íŋyaŋkA     yaŋkÁ     ištíŋmA     wótA     očhíŋšičA

Šúŋka waŋ ištíŋma čha waŋbláke.

Šúŋka waŋ _____ čha waŋbláke.     Šúŋka waŋ _____ čha waŋbláke.

Šúŋka waŋ _____ čha waŋbláke.     Šúŋka waŋ _____ čha waŋbláke.

**9 b** Look at the sentences you have written. Do ablaut verbs change their form before **čha**? Circle the correct answer: **Háŋ / Hiyá.**

**10 a** Let's look at some sentences with more information in them. Here are sentences about what Lisa sees in the camp. Can you match each of the people or animals in the column on the left with what they are doing on the right? Match them by drawing a line.

| | |
|---|---|
| **Wíŋyaŋ waŋ** | **čhéǧa waŋ yužáža.** |
| **Wičháša waŋ** | **pȟehíŋ kisúŋ.** |
| **Hokšíla waŋ** | **šúŋkawakȟáŋ waŋ wíyuŋ.** |
| **Kȟoškálaka waŋ** | **čháŋ pahí.** |
| **Wičháȟčala waŋ** | **čhaŋnúŋpa waŋ yuhá.** |
| **Šúŋka waŋ** | **maštíŋčala waŋ khuté.** |
| **Wíŋyaŋ waŋ** | **waŋhíŋkpe káǧe.** |
| **Wičhíŋčala waŋ** | **huhú waŋ yasmí.** |

**b** Now try joining two sentences together for yourself. Join the sentences using **čha**. Write a new, longer sentence for each example, like the model:

**Wíŋyaŋ waŋ čháŋ pahí.**   **Waŋbláke.**   _Wíŋyaŋ waŋ čháŋ pahí čha waŋbláke._

a) **Wičhíŋčala waŋ pȟehíŋ kisúŋ.**   **Waŋbláke.**   _____

b) **Hokšíla waŋ maštíŋčala waŋ khuté.**   **Waŋbláke.**   _____

č) **Kȟoškálaka waŋ waŋhíŋkpe káǧe.**   **Waŋbláke.**   _____

e) **Wíŋyaŋ waŋ čhéǧa waŋ yužáža.**   **Waŋbláke.**   _____

g) **Šúŋka waŋ huhú waŋ yasmí.**   **Waŋbláke.**   _____

 **11 a** Pretend that you are standing next to Lisa, looking at the camp. What do you see? On a piece of scratch paper, write 3 sentences, like the model.

**Hokšíla waŋ maštíŋčala waŋ khuté čha waŋbláke.**

**b** Now, read one of your sentences to your partner about what you see. He or she will point at the correct person or animal in the camp.

**Hokšíla waŋ maštíŋčala waŋ khuté čha waŋbláke.**

**12** Lisa made some drawings of her friends this weekend. What are her friends doing in the drawings? Make a sentence about one of the children following the model. Your classmate will guess which child you are talking about and point to the correct picture.

> **Hokšíla wáŋ wówapi waŋ yawá čha waŋbláke.**

**13** What happens when you see more than one animal or person?
Can you finish these sentences like the model?

**Ziŋtkála eyá kiŋyáŋpi čha** waŋwíčhablake.

a) **Šúŋkawakȟáŋ eyá wayášlapi čha** _____.

b) **Wičháša eyá kȟúl yaŋkápi čha** _____.

č) **Wičhíŋčala eyá takúku káǧapi** _____ _____.

e) **Hokšíla eyá wóglag yaŋkápi** _____ _____.

g) **Wakȟáŋheža eyá škátapi** _____ _____.

ǧ) **Wíŋyaŋ eyá wówaši ečhúŋpi** _____ _____.

**14** Summer needs help with her homework! Should she use **waŋbláke** or **waŋwíčhablake** in the sentences below? Can you help her fill in the correct word in each sentence?

**Wíŋyaŋ waŋ wakšú čha waŋbláke.**
**Wíŋyaŋ eyá wakšúpi čha waŋwíčhablake.**

**Wičháša waŋ waákhita čha** _____ .

**Šúŋkawakȟáŋ eyá íŋyaŋkapi čha** _____ .

**Wičhíŋčala eyá čhaŋk'íŋpi čha** _____ .

**Winúȟčala waŋ wakáǧeǧe čha** _____ .

**Kȟoškálaka eyá waŋhíŋkpe káǧapi čha** _____ .

**Wičháȟčala waŋ waníyetu iyáwapi waŋ káǧa čha** _____ .

**Wičháša eyá tȟaló pasnúŋpi čha** _____ .

**Wičhíŋčala waŋ čhéǧa waŋ yužáža čha** _____ .

**15** Make your own scene! Remember how Lisa talked about what she saw in the camp? Let's use that model to talk about your own drawing.

**a** First, on a piece of scratch paper, sketch at least 5 people or animals. Each one should be doing something: running, eating, reading a book etc. Next, write sentences about your drawing like the models.

Wičhíŋčala waŋ yawá čha waŋbláke.

Šúŋka waŋ wóta čha waŋbláke.

Wičhíŋčala waŋ wótȟaŋiŋ wówapi waŋ yawá čha waŋbláke.

Šúŋka waŋ huhú waŋ yúta čha waŋbláke.

**b** Now read the sentences out loud to your partner. DON'T show him/her your picture! Your partner will draw what you say on scratch paper. When you are done, compare your pictures! Did your partner understand what you said?

**16** What do you **remember**? Get into groups of three. Your teacher will quickly show you five pictures of people or animals doing things. With your team, write sentences about what you remember, like the model. The team that remembers the most gets a point!

Šúŋkawakȟáŋ kiŋ máni čha wéksuye.
Wičháša kiŋ zíškopela waŋ yúta čha wéksuye.

**17 a** What did you **see** on your way to school today? Write 3 sentences about what you noticed people or animals doing. Use the models to help you.

Hokšíla waŋ íŋyaŋka čha waŋbláke.
Wičháša waŋ wówapi ská pahí čha waŋbláke.

**b** Get in a circle with your classmates. First, you will say one of the sentences you wrote for activity 17a about what you noticed. Then, a classmate sitting next to you will report on what you say, like the models:

Hokšíla waŋ íŋyaŋka čha waŋbláke.

Hokšíla waŋ íŋyaŋka čha Tȟašína waŋyáŋke.

**Lisa uŋkíksuyapi kte héčha!**

**18** What happened to Lisa after she got to the village with Tȟaté Wiŋ? Skim the Coyote's story, and circle ALL the pictures that match what Lisa did at the village. Careful! Lisa may have done more than one thing.

Lisa Tȟaté Wiŋ húŋku kiŋ kičhí wóglaka čha waŋbláke. Tȟaté Wiŋ húŋku kiŋ Lisa wók'u čha waŋbláke. Lisa líla ȟčiŋ wóte šni čha awábleze. Lisa thiíkčeya waŋ thimá iyáya čha waŋbláke. Tȟaté Wiŋ húŋku kiŋ wiŋčhíŋčala kiŋ henáos ištíŋme-wičháši čha nawáȟ'uŋ. Lisa haŋp'íkčeka wakȟáŋ kiŋ ohán čha wéksuye. Uŋgnáš Lisa haŋp'íkčeka kiŋ uŋ thiyáta glí okíhi kte. Tókhel ilúkčaŋ so? Lisa thiyáta glí kta hwo?

**19** **a** What do you think is going to happen to Lisa? Do you think she will get home or not? Pick the sentence that you think is correct.

1) Lisa thiyáta khí kte.

2) Lisa čháŋthipi k'uŋ hé ektá khí kte.

3) Lisa eháŋni Lakȟóta wičhóthi kiŋ ektáni úŋ kte.

4) Lisa Ȟé Sápa ektá yíŋ kte.

**Tákuwe héčhel alúpta hwo?**

**b** Next, select the reason that Lisa will end up where you picked in the first part. Circle the best answer.

Lisa ikčéya iháŋble.

Haŋp'íkčeka kiŋ hená wakȟáŋ.

Haŋp'íkčeka kiŋ ikčéya eháŋni Lakȟóta wičhóthi kiŋ ektá aí.

**č** Then ask your classmates what their answers are. Do you all have the same opinion?

**Lisa tuktél yaŋká he?**

**Tákuwe héčhel alúpta he?**

**Lisa Lakȟóta wičhóthi kiŋ ektá yé šni. Thiyáta yaŋké.**

**Ikčéya iháŋble.**

**1** Skim through this dialogue. What does Lisa do that starts her time travel back to her own time? Circle the correct picture.

Tóhaŋ ȟčiŋ thiyáta wakhí kta he? Tȟaté-wiŋ na huŋku kiŋ waštéčakapi éyaš iná kičhí waúŋ šni čha iyómakišiče.

Itȟó haŋp'íkčeka kiŋ owáhiŋkte séče.

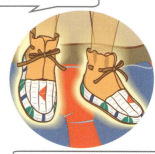

Lisa tókhiya iyáya hwo?

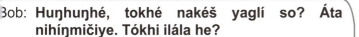

**Bob:** Huŋhuŋhé, tokhé nakéš yaglí so? Áta nihíŋmičiye. Tókhi ilála he?

**Lisa:** Tȟokéya obláye waŋ él nawážiŋ.

**Bob:** Hél tuwá waŋláka he?

**Lisa:** Eháŋk'ehaŋ wičhíŋčala waŋ waŋbláke kštó. Ho naháŋ oíglakiŋ na Tȟaté-wiŋ ečíyapi kéye. Wičhóthi waŋ ektá amái.

**Bob:** Táku isáŋp waŋláka he?

**Lisa:** Eháŋk'ehaŋ wičhóthi waŋ waŋbláke. Na él takúku óta waŋbláke kštó.

**Bob:** Wičhóthi kiŋ hé tuktél yaŋká he?

**Lisa:** Tuktél yaŋká héči slolwáye šni. Éyaš pahá waŋ iyóȟlathe yaŋké.

**Bob:** Tókheškhe yaglí he?

**Lisa:** Uŋčí tȟa-háŋp'ikčeka kiŋ owáhiŋ na uŋgnáhela tókhel waglí.

**Bob:** Haŋp'íkčeka kiŋ lená wakȟáŋ kéčhaŋmi yeló.

**2** Now, read the dialogue on page 29 again and circle the best answer to each of the questions below.

**a** **Lisa tókhiya í he?**

1) Otȟúŋwahe waŋ ektá í.

2) Obláye waŋ ektá í.

3) Čhúŋšoke waŋ ektá í.

4) Wakpá waŋ ektá í.

**b** **Lisa tuwá waŋyáŋka he?**

1) Lisa winúȟčala waŋ waŋyáŋke.

2) Lisa wičhíŋčala waŋ waŋyáŋke.

3) Lisa tuwéni waŋyáŋke šni.

4) Lisa kȟoškálaka waŋ waŋyáŋke.

**č** **Wičhóthi kiŋ tuktél yaŋká he?**

1) Blé waŋ ikhíyela yaŋké.

2) Pahá waŋ ikhíyela yaŋké.

3) Wakpá waŋ ikhíyela yaŋké.

4) Čhúŋšoke waŋ ikhíyela yaŋké.

**e** **Lisa táku waŋyáŋka he?**

1) Lisa táku óta waŋyáŋke.

2) Lisa táku čónala waŋyáŋke.

3) Lisa tákuni waŋyáŋke šni.

4) Lisa táku záptaŋ waŋyáŋke.

**g** **Lisa tókhel glí he?**

1) Nuŋwáŋpi uŋspé čha nuŋwáŋ glí.

2) Šuŋk'ákaŋyaŋg glí.

3) Haŋp'íkčeka wakȟáŋ kiŋ ohíŋ na uŋ glí.

4) Kiŋyékhiyapi waŋ ogná glí.

**3** ## Abléza po!

**Táku** can have different meanings in different sentences. Sometimes it means "what" and sometimes it means "something." Study the sentences below and then answer questions a) and b) that follow.

| | | | |
|---|---|---|---|
| **Táku waŋláka he?** | What do you see? | **Táku waŋbláke.** | I see something. |
| **Táku iyáču he?** | What did you take? | **Táku iwáču.** | I took something. |
| **Táku nič'ú he?** | What did he give you? | **Táku mak'ú.** | He gave me something. |
| **Táku nayáȟ'uŋ he?** | What do you hear? | **Táku nawáȟ'uŋ.** | I hear something. |
| **Táku oyále he?** | What are you looking for? | **Táku owále.** | I am looking for something. |

**a** Does **táku** mean "something" in a question, or in an answer? Circle the best choice:

Question          Answer

**b** What does **táku** mean in the questions above? Circle the best choice:

What          Something

**4** Work with a partner. One of you will select a picture, but don't tell your partner! Your partner will ask a question to figure out which picture you picked, like the model:

**Táku waŋláka he?**

**Táku kiŋyáŋ čha waŋbláke.**

**Lé ziŋtkála é!**

**5** Some other words work the same way as **táku**. **Tóna** and **tuwá** can mean different things in different sentences too. Look at the sentences below. Draw lines to match the Lakota sentences with the English equivalent.

| | |
|---|---|
| **Tuwá waŋbláke.** | I saw several. |
| **Tuwá waŋláka he?** | How many did you see? |
| **Tóna waŋbláke.** | Who did you see? |
| **Tóna waŋláka he?** | I saw someone. |

**6** Here are some text messages with pictures that Summer and Lisa sent each other, but some of the words are missing! Can you fill in the correct words? Use **tóna**, **tuwá** or **táku**. Use each word only once!

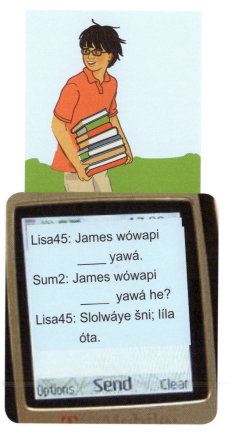

Sum2: Mathó _____ yuhá.
Lisa45: Mathó _____ yuhá he?
Sum2: Slolwáye šni; ophíye ogná yaŋké.

Sum2: Bob _____ napéyuze.
Lisa45: Bob _____ napéyuza he?
Sum2: Slolwáye šni.

Lisa45: James wówapi _____ yawá.
Sum2: James wówapi _____ yawá he?
Lisa45: Slolwáye šni; líla óta.

**7 a** Now, working with a partner, choose a picture. Your partner will again ask questions, this time using **táku** and **tóna**, to figure out which picture you chose, like the model.

Táku waŋláka he?

Tóna waŋláka he?

Lé ičítopa é!

Wakšíča kiŋ waŋbláke.

Waŋžíla waŋbláke. / Tóna waŋbláke.

 1
 2
 3
 4
 5
 6
 7
 8

**7 b** Work with your partner again. Choose one of the pictures below. Your partner will try to guess which picture you chose by asking questions, like the model:

Tuwá waŋláka he?

Wičháša kiŋ waŋbláke.

Lé ičítopa é!

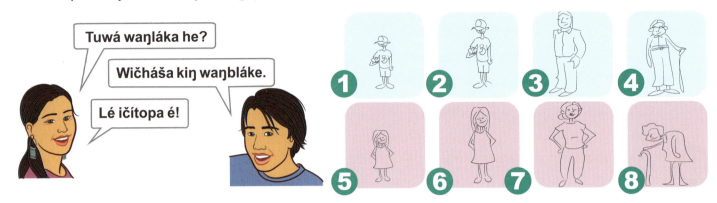

**8 a** I see someone running. I see someone walking! First draw a picture with several people doing different things that you know how to say in Lakota. Then, on a piece of scrap paper write sentences about your picture like the models. Write at least 4 sentences.

Tuwá nuŋwáŋ čha waŋbláke. Tuwá máni čha waŋbláke.
Tuwá psíča čha waŋbláke. Tuwá šuŋk'ákaŋyaŋka čha waŋbláke.

**b** Now work with a partner. Read your sentences to your partner. Your partner will draw what he/she hears. When you are finished, compare your partner's drawing with your original drawing. Did he/she understand what you said?

**9** Which animals do you see? Work with a partner again. Choose a picture, but don't tell your partner! Your partner will ask questions, this time using **táku** and **tóna**, to figure out which picture you chose, like the model.

Táku waŋláka he?

Tȟatȟáŋka kiŋ waŋwíčhablake.

Tóna waŋwíčhalaka he?

Tóna waŋwíčhablake. /
Núŋpa waŋwíčhablake.

Lé ičíyamni é!

## 10 Abléza po!

We have learned that **táku**, **tóna** and **tuwá** each have two different meanings. But we can't use **tuwá, tóna** and **táku** in negative sentences. Look at the sentences below. For each of the "t" words we have talked about, find the word you would use in a negative sentence.

| Question | Positive | Negative |
|---|---|---|
| Táku waŋláka he? | Táku waŋbláke. | Tákuni waŋbláke šni. |
| Tuwá waŋláka he? | Tuwá waŋbláke. | Tuwéni waŋbláke šni. |
| Tóna waŋláka he? | Tóna waŋbláke. | Waŋžíni waŋbláke šni. |

**11** James is doing his homework. Can you help him? Look at the sentences below, and draw lines to match the question to the positive sentence and then to the corresponding negative sentence, like the model.

| | | |
|---|---|---|
| Táku waŋláka he? | Tuwá pȟóskil blúze. | Tákuni owále šni. |
| Tuwá waŋláka he? | Tóna opȟéwatȟuŋ. | Tuwéni pȟóskil blúze šni. |
| Tóna waŋláka he? | Tóna waŋbláke. | Waŋžíni opȟéwatȟuŋ šni. |
| Táku nič'ú he? | Táku waŋbláke. | Waŋžíni waŋbláke šni. |
| Tuwá nayáȟ'uŋ he? | Tuwá nawáȟ'uŋ. | Tákuni waŋbláke šni. |
| Tóna luhá he? | Tóna bluhá. | Tuwéni waŋbláke šni. |
| Táku oyále he? | Tuwá waŋbláke. | Waŋžíni bluhá šni. |
| Tuwá pȟóskil lúza he? | Táku owále. | Tákuni mak'ú šni. |
| Tóna opȟéyatȟuŋ he? | Táku mak'ú. | Tuwéni nawáȟ'uŋ šni. |

**12** You have been asked to make a list of everything in this storage shed! To save time, work with a partner. Each of you will take half the building. Partner one looks at the picture on page 141 and partner two looks at the picture on page 142. **Write down what is on every shelf in your half of the building.**

**a** First, look at your own half of the building, and write sentences about what you see.

> Wíkȟaŋ waŋ waŋbláke.
>
> Matȟó yámni waŋwíčhablake.

**b** Next, ask your partner about each shelf in his/her section. Does s/he see anything? What does s/he see? Use the model to help you. **Fill in the empty half of your building map with what your partner tells you.**

> Akáŋwaeglepi ičínuŋpa kiŋ akáŋl táku waŋží waŋláka he?

> Háŋ, táku waŋbláke.

> Hé táku é?

> Wíyatke tóna waŋbláke.

**13** Someone drew a big smiley face on your classroom wall! But you didn't see anything! Your teacher is asking you questions about it. Answer all of the questions negatively.

Tuwá waŋláka he? ⟶ Tuwéni waŋbláke šni.

Tuwá nayáȟ'uŋ he?

Táku ayábleza he?

Táku itóyawa he?

Wíčazo tóna luhá he?

Tóna yakázo he?

## 14 Abléza po!

In Lakota, there is more than one way to say "something." You already know how to use "**táku**." But there is another way to say "something" : "**takúŋl**." Read the sentences below, and circle the correct answer for each question.

**Híŋhaŋni líla lowáčhiŋ čha táku wáte.**

**Mázaska eyá bluhá čha ȟtálehaŋ mas'óphiye-ta táku opȟéwatȟuŋ.**

**Híŋhaŋni kiŋ mas'óphiye-ta blé háŋtaŋš takúŋl opȟéwatȟuŋ kte.**

**Lowáčhiŋ kiŋháŋ takúŋl wátiŋ kte.**

1. Which one is used to talk about something that is happening or has already happened? **táku / takúŋl**
2. Which one is used to talk about something that might or will happen? **táku / takúŋl**

**15** Stand in a circle with your classmates. You are going to play **Iktómi kéye** (like Simon Says)!

Tuwá ayúta ye/yo!

Tuwá wókiyaka yo/ye!

Tuwá mas'ákipȟa ye/yo!

Tuwá pȟóskil yúza ye/yo!

Tuwá napéyuza ye/yo!

Tuwá yuš'íŋyeya ye/yo!

Takúŋl yúta ye/yo!

Takúŋl yatkáŋ ye/yo!

Takúŋl ahíyaya ye/yo!

Takúŋl pahí ye/yo!

Takúŋl ikíkču we/wo!

Takúŋl owá ye/yo!

Tuwá takúŋl kipázo we/wo!

Tuwá takúŋl k'ú we/wo!

Iktómi kéye, takúŋl yatkáŋ ye!

Takúŋl yatkáŋ ye.

Bob é na Lisa táku tókȟuŋpi he?

**16** Bob and Lisa are still in grandma's log cabin, looking at things. Skim through the story below. Then circle the verb that best describes how they feel right now.

Nihíŋčiyapi     Iyókiphipi     Čhaŋzékapi     Čhaŋtéšičapi

Lisa: **Thiókaȟmi kiŋ etáŋhaŋ takúŋl nayáȟ'uŋ he?**

Bob: **Tákuni nawáȟ'uŋ šni.**

Lisa: **Anáǧoptaŋ ye! Kál táku škaŋškáŋ s'elél. Hé táku he? Uŋgnáš zuzéča héčha séče.**

Bob: **Waȟnáš nawáȟ'uŋ, éyaš thimáhetaŋhaŋ nawáȟ'uŋ šni. Tuwá tȟaŋkál ománi s'eléčheča!**

Lisa: **Tóhaŋni tuwéni hí šni. Éeye matȟópi kéčhaŋmi.**

Bob: **Wičáyakȟe ló. Matȟó kiŋ tónapi he? Tȟaŋkál éyouŋkas'iŋ héči!**

Lisa: **Matȟó waŋžíni waŋbláke šni. Éeye zičáȟota eyá psíčapi čha waŋwíčhablake. Líla hótȟaŋkiŋkiŋyaŋpi!**

**17**  **a** First, look through the questions and underline any words you don't know. Look them up in the dictionary and draw a little picture next to each word to help you remember the meaning.

**b** Then, read the dialogue above, and circle the best answer for each question below.

Lisa táku naȟ'úŋ. Tuktétaŋhaŋ hiyú he?

1) Thiókaȟmi kiŋ etáŋhaŋ táku naȟ'úŋ. 2) Tȟaŋkátaŋhaŋ táku naȟ'úŋ. 3) Čhaŋyátaŋhaŋ táku naȟ'úŋ.

Bob tȟoká táku naȟ'úŋ he?

1) Maštíŋčala waŋ naȟ'úŋ. 2) Tákuni naȟ'úŋ šni. 3) Tȟaté kiŋ naȟ'úŋ šni.

Lisa íŋš-eyá táku naȟ'úŋ he?

1) Háŋ, maštíŋčala waŋ naȟ'úŋ. 2) Hiyá, tákuni naȟ'úŋ šni. 3) Háŋ, tȟaté kiŋ naȟ'úŋ.

Bob táku naȟ'úŋ. <u>Zuzéča</u> kéčhiŋ he?

1) Hiyá, waȟpé kasnásna čha naȟ'úŋ kéčhiŋ. 2) Hiyá, tȟaté hiyú čha naȟ'úŋ kéčhiŋ.

3) Hiyá, tuwá tȟaŋkál ománi čha naȟ'úŋ kéčhiŋ.

Lisa matȟó héčhapi kéčhiŋ. Matȟó kiŋ tónapi he?

1) Matȟó kiŋ núŋpapi. 2) Matȟó kiŋ šakówiŋpi. 3) Hél matȟó waŋžíni nážiŋ šni.

Čha heháŋl Bob é na L[...] táku akhípȟapi kta hwo? Haŋp'íkčeka k'uŋ hé íŋš tó[...]

Lisa é na Bob tȟaŋkál éyokas'iŋpi yuŋkȟáŋ táku waŋyáŋkapi he?

1) Ziŋtkála núŋpapi čha waŋwíčhayaŋkapi. 2) Zičáȟota núŋpapi čha waŋwíčhayaŋkapi.

3) Tákuni waŋyáŋkapi šni.

**1** Skim through the story below. When Bob puts on the moccasins, where does he go? Circle the correct picture.

**2** Now skim through the part of the story on the next page. What has happened in the village? Circle the correct picture.

Haŋp'íkčeka kiŋ owáhe háŋtaŋš míš-eyá eháŋk'ehaŋ wičhóthi kiŋ ektá mníŋ kta he?

Uŋgnáš! Ho éyaš líla wókȟokipȟe s'eléčheča. Uŋgná yakú kte šni séče.

Iníhaŋšni ečhámuŋ kte. Míš-eyá wičhóthi kiŋ waŋbláka wačhíŋ yeló.

Waŋná íŋš heháŋtu.....Bob wičhóthi kiŋ ektá yíŋ kta hwo? Glí kta hwo?

Huŋhuŋhé! Tuktél wahínažiŋ he? Eháŋk'ehaŋ Lakȟól wičhóuŋ kiŋ lél wahí séče. Wáŋ, ká hokšíla waŋ máni ú kiŋ hé tuwé he?

Míš, Tȟaté-wiŋ thiblóku miyé. Míla Kič'úŋ emáčiyapi.

Bob emáčiyapi. Tókȟa čha oyáte kiŋ iglág éyaya he? Tákuwe?

Tokhé yahí so? Wówiȟaya niglúze, wičhíŋčala waŋ Lisa ečíyapi kiŋ slolyáye séče.

Háŋ, Lisa haŋkášiwaye ló.

Míla Kič'úŋ: **Hékta yámni-čhaŋ k'uŋ héhaŋ wašíču akíčhita eyá natáŋ uŋkáhiyupi.**

Bob: **Tákuwe čha héčhuŋpi he?**

Míla Kič'úŋ: **Slolwáye šni. Oyáte kiŋ naúŋkič'ižiŋpi yuŋkȟáŋ haŋkéya ȟeyáb iyáyapi. Ho k'éyaš wašíču kiŋ uŋgnáš kúpi kte ló.**

Bob: **Níš, ób níŋ kta he?**

Míla Kič'úŋ: **Háŋ, ób mníŋ kte, ičhíŋ thiyóšpaye kiŋ hé ómapȟa.**

Bob: **Míš-eyá ób mníŋ kta wačhíŋ. Iȟpéya imáyaye šni yo, mišnála nawážiŋ wačhíŋ šni.**

Míla Kič'úŋ: **Takómni! Hiyú wo.**

**3** Go through the story again and then choose the best answer for each question below.

**a** Bob haŋp'íkčeka kiŋ ohíŋ kte, éyaš Lisa wičǎla šni. Tákuwe?
1) Wayázaŋ kta kéčhiŋ.
2) Haŋp'íkčeka kiŋ šapšápiŋ kta kéčhiŋ.
3) Thiyáta glí kte šni kéčhiŋ.

**b** Tákuwe Bob haŋp'íkčeka kiŋ ohíŋ kta čhíŋ he?
1) Ičhíŋ sí kiŋ snisní.
2) Wičhóthi kiŋ waŋyáŋkiŋ kte ȟčiŋ.
3) Ičhíŋ zičá wičhákhuwa kte.

**č** Míla Kič'úŋ ečíyapi kiŋ hé tuwé he?
1) Tȟaté Wiŋ thiblóku.
2) Bob tȟaŋháŋšitku.
3) Lisa tȟuŋwíŋču kiŋ čhiŋkšítku.

**e** Lakȟóta oyáte kiŋ táku tókȟuŋpi kta iglúwiŋyeyapi he?
1) Iglág iyáyapi kta iglúwiŋyeyapi.
2) Lol'íȟ'aŋpi kta iglúwiŋyeyapi.
3) Wačhípi kta iglúwiŋyeyapi.

**g** Hékta yámni-čhaŋ k'uŋ héhaŋ táku tókȟa he?
1) Šuŋgmánitu tȟáŋka eyá wičhóthi kiŋ anátaŋpi.
2) Wašíču akíčhita eyá wičhóthi kiŋ anátaŋpi.
3) Šahíyela eyá wičhóthi kiŋ anátaŋpi.

**ǧ** Oyáte kiŋ tákuwe iglákapi kta he?
1) Wóyute ignípi kta čha iglákapi kte.
2) Nuŋwáŋpi kta čha iglákapi kte.
3) Wašíču kiŋ akhé kúpi kta kéčhiŋpi kiŋ uŋ iglákapi kte.

**h** Bob tákuwe Míla Kič'úŋ kičhí yá čhíŋ he?
1) Išnála úŋ čhíŋ šni.
2) Thiyáta glá čhíŋ šni.
3) Wičhóthi kiŋ waŋyáŋka čhíŋ šni.

**4** **a** Take a look at the people from the village (on the following page) as they are on the move from one campsite to another. People are doing lots of different things. A lot of them are walking. Some of them are riding. Look at the chart below to see how to talk about portions of a group, like "some of the..." or "many of the...". Then do the exercise that follows the chart.

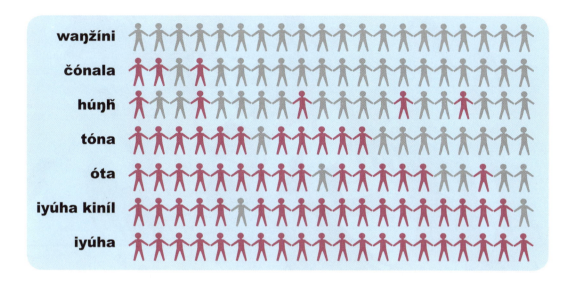

**b** Read the sentences and look at the icons. Finish the sentences using the correct word to say what part or portion of the people or animals are doing each thing. Use the chart above to help you.

**wanžíni // tóna // čónala // húŋȟ // óta // iyúha kiníl // iyúha**

1) Šúŋkawakȟáŋ kiŋ  iyúha  íŋyaŋkapi.

2) Wičháša kiŋ _____ šuŋkʼákaŋyaŋkapi.

3) Šúŋka kiŋ _____ mánipi.

4) Šuŋka kiŋ _____ kichizapi.

5) Hokšíla kiŋ _____ šuŋkʼákaŋyaŋkapi.

6) Šúŋka kiŋ _____ wapȟápȟapi.

7) Wíŋyaŋ kiŋ _____ íŋyaŋkapi.

8) Wičhíŋčala kiŋ _____ mánipi.

**5** Look at the picture on the next page, and then look over the sentences you just finished. How many of them are true about the picture? Put a check mark next to each of the sentences that is true.

**6** **a** Look back at the picture of the camp on the move! Can you write 3 more sentences about what you see? What are some of the dogs doing? What are all the horses doing? What are many of the boys doing? What are none of the girls doing? Use the sentences of 4b as a model.

**b** Read your sentences to your partner. Your partner will sketch what he/she hears. When you are done, look at your partner's sketch. Did he or she understand you? How does the sketch compare to the original drawing?

**7** You and your partner are planning to have some friends over, and you need to buy some food and drinks. You are inviting 10 people. Your teacher will give you each a list of what your friends like and don't like. Don't show your list to your partner!

Na níš tók? Na uŋmá wayáwa kiŋ hená íŋš tók? Toháŋl šna wítaya mniníčiyapi kiŋ táku yúl awášteyalakapi hwo? Táku yatkáŋ awášteyalakapi hwo?

**a** First look at the information the teacher gave you and write some sentences about what your friends like or don't like, like the model.

Waŋžíni wašíŋska waštélake šni
Čónala uŋžíŋžiŋtka haŋpí waštélakapi.
Húŋȟ wasná waštélakapi.
Tóna psíŋ waštélakapi.
Iyúha kiníl wóžapi waštélakapi.

**b** Next, read your sentences to your partner. You partner should make some notes about how many people like each item.

**8** Now, with your partner, talk about how much of each item you should buy. Circle the best basket to buy for your party.

Iyúha kiníl tȟaspáŋ waštélakapi!

Oháŋ, čha tȟaspáŋ óta opȟéuŋtȟuŋ kte!

Waŋžíni wagmúšpaŋšni waštélake šni.

Wičáyakȟe, čha wagmúšpaŋšni waŋžíni opȟéuŋtȟuŋ kte šni.

Tóna tȟaspáŋhaŋpi waštélakapi.

Oháŋ, čha tȟaspáŋhaŋpi etáŋ opȟéuŋtȟuŋ kte.

# 9 | Abléza po!

There is more than one way to say "some of the" in Lakota. Some sentences talk about items you can count, like apples and oranges. Other sentences talk about things that you don't count, like meat and tea. Look at the sentences and answer the questions.

How do you say "some of the..." when you are talking about something you count?     **húŋȟ     haŋké**

How do you say "some of the ..." when you are talking about something you don't count?     **húŋȟ     haŋké**

**Tȟaló kiŋ haŋké wačhíŋ.**

**Wagmúšpaŋšni kiŋ haŋké wáte.**

**Tȟaspáŋ opémnipi kiŋ haŋké iwáču.**

**Tȟaspáŋ kiŋ húŋȟ wačhíŋ.**

**Mnikápȟopapi kiŋ húŋȟ blatké.**

**Čaŋmháŋska kiŋ húŋȟ wáte.**

**10** Summer and Tȟašína had a party too! Their party was great! Their friends brought some of their favorite foods to eat. But now it's clean-up time, and they're checking to see how much of each food is left.

Read the dialogue below, and finish drawing and coloring the pictures to show who ate how much of which food, like the model.

Summer: **Wáŋ k'éya! James tȟaló kiŋ áta tȟebyé.**

Tȟašína: **Hiyá, James tȟebyé šni. Matȟó íŋš-eyá tȟaló kiŋ haŋké yúte.**

Summer: **Lé wagmúšpaŋšni kiŋ líla wašté! Óta wáte.**

Tȟašína: **Míš-eyá wagmúšpaŋšni kiŋ haŋké wáte.**

Summer: **Kimi tȟaspáŋ kiŋ húŋȟ yúta he?**

Tȟašína: **Háŋ, tȟaspáŋ kiŋ húŋȟ yútiŋ na nakúŋ psíŋ kiŋ húŋȟ yúte. Maštíŋčala s'e wóte s'a!**

Summer: **Mike táku yúta he?**

Tȟašína: **Mike kȟáŋta kiŋ húŋȟ yútiŋ na pápa kiŋ óta yútiŋ na tȟaspáŋ opémnipi kiŋ haŋké yúte.**

Summer: **Míš-eyá tȟaspáŋ opémnipi kiŋ haŋké wáte.**

Tȟašína: **Míš-eyá! Tȟaspáŋ opémnipi kiŋ átaya tȟebyápi.**

Summer: **Éyaš tuwéni omníča kiŋ etáŋhaŋ yúte šni!**

| James | Kimi | Matȟó | Tȟašína | Summer | Mike |
|---|---|---|---|---|---|
|  |  |  |  |  |  |
| |  | |  |  |  |

**11** Like many other words we have learned, **húŋȟ** and **haŋké** are not used in negative sentences. Read the mini-dialogues below. Then, figure out what word you would use to reply negatively to each of these words, and write it in the blank following the word.

**Húŋȟ** ---> _____          **Haŋké** ---> _____

Tȟaspáŋ kiŋ húŋȟ yačhíŋ he?

Hiyá, tȟaspáŋ kiŋ huŋǧéni wačhíŋ šni.

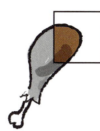

Tȟaló kiŋ haŋké yačhíŋ he?

Hiyá, tȟaló kiŋ haŋkéni wačhíŋ šni.

Tȟaspáŋ opémnipi kiŋ haŋké yačhíŋ he?

Hiyá, tȟaspáŋ opémnipi kiŋ haŋkéni wačhíŋ šni.

Tȟaspáŋpȟestola kiŋ húŋȟ yačhíŋ he?

Hiyá, tȟaspáŋpȟestola kiŋ huŋǧéni wačhíŋ šni.

**12** Kimi is helping her aunt with her shopping. Can you finish their dialogue below? Use **húŋȟ**, **huŋǧéni**, **haŋké**, or **haŋkéni**.

Kimi: **Tȟuŋwíŋ, uŋžíŋžiŋtka kiŋ _____ yačhíŋ he?**

Kimi Tȟuŋwíŋču: **Hiyá, uŋžíŋžiŋtka kiŋ _____ wačhíŋ šni. Tuwéni waštélake šni!**

Kimi: **Tȟaló kiŋ _____ yačhíŋ he?**

Kimi Tȟuŋwíŋču: **Hiyá, tȟaló kiŋ _____ wačhíŋ šni. Thiyáta tȟaló óta uŋglúhapi.**

Kimi: **Tȟuŋwíŋ, asáŋpi sutá kiŋ _____ yačhíŋ he?**

Kimi Tȟuŋwíŋču: **Háŋ, _____ wačhíŋ. Iyúha asáŋpi sutá waštélakapi.**

Kimi Tȟuŋwíŋču: **Háš! Kȟáŋta kiŋ éwektuŋže!**

**Tȟožáŋ, kȟáŋta šašá kiŋ _____ imákiču yé.**

Kimi: **Oháŋ, tȟuŋwíŋ, kȟáŋta kiŋ _____ ičhíčiču kte.**

**13** You and your class are going to the fair! Some of you will be selling food at the fair. Your teacher will give you a card with the food you are selling on it. Some of you will be buying food! Walk around, see what the sellers have, and make your choices. Talk to the sellers, like the model, and then make a list of what you want! You can only choose 3 things in total.

Tȟaspáŋ kiŋ lená líla waštéšte! Húŋȟ yačhíŋ he?

Háŋ, húŋȟ wačhíŋ.

Hiyá, huŋǧéni wačhíŋ šni.

Hiyá, haŋkéni wačhíŋ šni.

Pápa kiŋ lé líla wašté. Haŋké yačhíŋ he?

Háŋ, haŋké wačhíŋ.

**14** **Abléza po!**

Some items can be both countable and uncountable depending on the situation. Look at these examples:

1. Tȟaspáŋ kiŋ húŋȟ wačhíŋ.

2. Tȟaspáŋ kiŋ haŋké wačhíŋ.

In which sentence are we talking about some of the many?    **sentence 1   sentence 2**

In which sentence are we talking about some of a larger, uncountable whole?    **sentence 1   sentence 2**

**15** Look at what the children are saying that they are eating or drinking. Draw lines to match what they say with the correct pictures.

Summer: **Zíškopela kiŋ haŋké wačhíŋ.**

Lisa: **Zíškopela kiŋ húŋȟ uŋkíkičupi ye.**

Kimi: **Tȟaspáŋ kiŋ haŋké tȟebwáye.**

Mike: **Tȟaspáŋ kiŋ húŋȟ uŋyútapi.**

James: **Tȟaspáŋ opémnipi kiŋ haŋké wačhíŋ.**

Matȟó: **Tȟaspáŋ opémnipi kiŋ húŋȟ Bob kičhí tȟeb'úŋyaŋpi.**

Tȟašína: **Čhaŋmháŋska ǧí kiŋ haŋké imákiču.**

Mike: **Čhaŋmháŋska ǧí kiŋ húŋȟ tȟebčhíčhiye!**

**16** Look at the sentences and pictures below. Finish the sentences using **húŋȟ** or **haŋké**, depending on what the picture suggests.

Bló kiŋ _____ opȟéyatȟuŋ he?

Wagmúšpaŋšni kiŋ _____ opȟéuŋtȟuŋ kte! Líla waštéšte!

Blopátȟaŋpi kiŋ _____ tȟebyáya he?

Wagmúšpaŋšni kiŋ _____ wáta wačhíŋ! Líla lowáčhiŋ!

Čhaŋmháŋska ǧí kiŋ _____ ičú ye.

Pȟaŋǧí-zizí kiŋ _____ iwáču kte.

Čhaŋmháŋska ǧí kiŋ _____ čhičíyute.

Pȟaŋǧí-zizí kiŋ _____ iwáču kte.

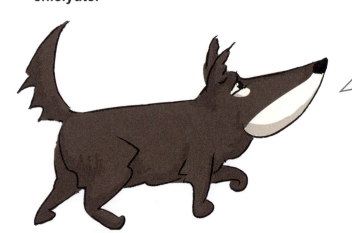

Bob waŋná tuktél úŋ he? Míla Kič'úŋ tȟa-óyate
ób ektáni úŋ kta he? Éwaŋuŋyaŋkapi kte!
Uŋgnáš wóuŋspe íyokhihe kiŋ hetáŋhaŋ
éslol'uŋyaŋpi kte!

**1** Skim through the dialogue below, look at the pictures, and circle the correct answer to the question.

Tuwá Bob kičhí wóglaka he?
a. wičháša itháŋčhaŋ    b. Lisa atkúku    č. Lekšítku

Bob: **Tóhaŋ tȟóka kiŋ hená hípi he?**

Tȟašúŋke-Ská: Hékta tópa-čhaŋ k'uŋ héhaŋ léčhiya hípi. Uŋgnáhela wičhóthi kiŋ ogná šuŋk'ákaŋyaŋg hípi.

Bob: **Líla wókȟokipȟeke! Heháŋl táku tókȟuŋpi he?**

Tȟašúŋke-Ská: Wičhúŋkhutepi čha napȟápi.

Bob: **Tóhaŋ ničhíye kiŋ thiíkčeya kiŋ ilékhiyapi he?**

Tȟašúŋke-Ská: Napȟápi šni haŋní iléyapi.

Bob: **Tóhaŋ tȟokéya wašíču kiŋ waŋwíčhalakapi he?**

Tȟašúŋke-Ská: Tȟuŋkášilawaya waŋ tȟokéya waŋwíčhayaŋke.

Bob: **Kaíyuzeya maúŋnipi só. Toháŋl éuŋthipi kta he?**

Tȟašúŋke-Ská: Blihíč'iya yo! Wí mahél iyáye šni haŋní éuŋthipi kte.

Bob: **Toháŋl waúŋyutapi kta he?**

Tȟašúŋke-Ská: Éuŋthipi kiŋháŋ heháŋl waúŋyutapi kte. Kaíyuzeya uŋkípi kiŋháŋ éuŋthipi kte.

Bob: **Híŋhaŋni kiŋháŋ watóhaŋl iglág uŋkíyayapi kta he?**

Tȟašúŋke-Ská: Wí hinápȟe kiŋháŋ uŋkíyayapi kte.

**2** Read the dialogue on page 49 again, and then answer these questions:

1. Tȟóka kiŋ hená tóhaŋ wičhóthi kiŋ ektá hípi he?
   a. Hékta yámni-čhaŋ k'uŋ héhaŋ.
   b. Hékta óta-čhaŋ k'uŋ héhaŋ.
   č. Hékta tópa-čhaŋ k'uŋ héhaŋ.

2. Tuktél šuŋk'ákaŋyaŋkapi he?
   a. Wičhóthi kiŋ ohómni šuŋk'ákaŋyaŋkapi.
   b. Wičhóthi kiŋ aínab šuŋk'ákaŋyaŋkapi.
   č. Wičhóthi kiŋ égna šuŋk'ákaŋyaŋkapi.

3. Lakȟóta kiŋ táku tókȟuŋpi he?
   a. Lakȟóta kiŋ napȟápi.
   b. Lakȟóta kiŋ šuŋk'ákaŋyaŋkapi.
   č. Lakȟóta kiŋ wašíču kiŋ wičhákhutepi.

4. Tóhaŋ Tȟašúŋke-Ská čhiyéku kiŋ tȟíikčeya kiŋ ilékhiyapi he?
   a. Ȟtayétu iléyapi.
   b. Tȟokáta aŋpétu waŋží iléyapi kte.
   č. Iyáyapi šni haŋní iléyapi.

5. Tóhaŋ oyáte kiŋ wašíču kiŋ tȟokéya waŋwíčhayaŋkapi he?
   a. Ȟtálehaŋ. b. Lečhála. č. Eháŋni.

6. Oyáte kiŋ toháŋl éthipi kta he?
   a. Letáŋhaŋ núŋpa-čhaŋ kiŋháŋ.
   b. Híŋhaŋni kiŋháŋ.
   č. Wí mahél iyáye šni haŋní.

7. Oyáte kiŋ toháŋl wótapi kta he?
   a. Éthipi šni haŋni wótapi kte.
   b. Éthipi kiŋháŋ wótapi kte.
   č. Asníkiyapi kiŋháŋ wótapi kte.

8. Oyáte kiŋ toháŋl akhé iglág iyáyapi kta he?
   a. Letáŋhaŋ núŋpa-čháŋ kiŋháŋ.
   b. Haŋhépi kiŋháŋ.
   č. Wí hinápȟe kiŋháŋ heháŋl.

**3** ## Abléza po!

In Lakota there are two ways to say "when". Read the examples and see if you can figure out the difference.

Tóhaŋ yahí he?

Híŋhaŋni wahí.

Toháŋl Denver-ta níŋ kta he?

Híŋhaŋni kiŋháŋ Denver-ta mníŋ kte.

Tóhaŋ Bob waŋláka he?

Ȟtálehaŋ Bob waŋbláke.

Toháŋl yaglí kta he?

Tȟokáta okó kiŋháŋ waglí kte.

Circle the best choice:

a) **Tóhaŋ** is used for things that already happened. **Toháŋl** is used for things that will or might happen.

b) **Toháŋl** is used for things that already happened. **Tóhaŋ** is used for things that will or might happen.

č) **Toháŋl** is used by boys or men and **tóhaŋ** is used by girls or women.

**4** Now let's look at these questions from Bob's conversation with Tȟašúŋke-Ska. In which of the questions are they talking about something that already happened? Circle them! In which of the questions are they talking about something that might or will happen? Underline them!

Tóhaŋ tȟóka kiŋ hípi he?                    Toháŋl éuŋthipi kta he?

Tóhaŋ thiíkčeya kiŋ iléyapi he?              Toháŋl waúŋyutapi kta he?

Tóhaŋ wašíču kiŋ tȟokéya waŋwíčhayaŋkapi he?    Toháŋl akhé iglág uŋkíyayapi kta he?

**5** Kimi and Mike want to interview their classmates about some of the activities they did last weekend, and what they are planning to do this coming weekend. Can you help them finish the interview questions? Use **tóhaŋ** or **toháŋl**.

1. Hékta Owáŋkayužažapi k'uŋ héhaŋ _____ yékta he?

2. Hékta Owáŋkayužažapi k'uŋ héhaŋ _____ inúŋka he?

3. Hékta Aŋpétuwakȟáŋ k'uŋ héhaŋ _____ ȟtawáyata he?

4. Hékta Aŋpétuwakȟáŋ k'uŋ héhaŋ _____ inúŋka he?

5. _____ Owáŋkayužažapi yékta kiŋháŋ tȟokáheya táku tókȟanuŋ kta he?

6. _____ otȟúŋwahe-ta níŋ kta he?

7. _____ wayátiŋ kta he?

8. Nitȟákȟola / Nitȟámaške kiŋ _____ waŋyéglakiŋ kta he?

**6** Bob and Lisa are really busy this weekend! Can you figure out their schedules? Pretend that it is Saturday night now. Work with a partner. One of you will look at Lisa's schedule on page 141, and one of you will look at Bob's schedule on page 142. Ask your partner questions to fill in the time for each of Bob and Lisa's activities.

> Lisa tóhaŋ nuŋwáŋ he?

> Lisa hékta owápȟe napčíyuŋka k'uŋ héhaŋ nuŋwé.

> Lisa toháŋl wakšú kta he?

> Lisa owápȟe akéwaŋži kiŋháŋ wakšú kte.

Here are Lisa's activities.

Lisa Saturday:          Lisa Sunday:

 _____     _____

_____     _____

_____    _____

Here are Bob's activities.

Bob Saturday:          Bob Sunday:

 _____     _____

 _____     _____

 _____     _____

**7** You want to do the same survey that Kimi and Mike did in activity 5, about what your classmates did last weekend, and what they are planning to do this weekend. Talk to two people in your class, and ask the same questions that Kimi and Mike did. Fill in the chart with the answers.

> Hékta Owáŋkayužažapi k'uŋ héhaŋ _____ yékta he?

> Owápȟe šakówiŋ k'uŋ héhaŋ wékta.

> Toháŋl otȟúŋwahe-ta níŋ kta he?

> Owápȟe napčíyuŋka kiŋháŋ otȟúŋwahe-ta mníŋ kte.

| Wówiyuŋǧe | čhažé | | čhažé | |
|---|---|---|---|---|
| 1 | | | | |
| 2 | | | | |
| 3 | | | | |
| 4 | | | | |
| 5 | | | | |
| 6 | | | | |
| 7 | | | | |
| 8 | | | | |

**8** Now, let's see how much you remember about what your classmates did last weekend and will do this weekend! Write 4 sentences about your classmates' answers to the questions you asked, like the models.

Hékta Aŋpétuwakȟáŋ k'uŋ héhaŋ Cynthia owápȟe wikčémna k'uŋ héhaŋ kiktá.
Cynthia owápȟe záptaŋ kiŋháŋ otȟúŋwahe-ta yíŋ kte.

_____

_____

_____

**9** Bob and Lisa have invited some of their friends to join them. Now, they are telling Lisa's mother what their plans are. Can you match each of the sentences with the correct picture? How many of these activities do you remember?

1. **Tȟokáta Owáŋkayužažapi kiŋháŋ, owápȟe núŋpa kiŋháŋ uŋnúŋwaŋpi kte.**

2. **Heháŋl pteyúha othí kiŋ ektá uŋyáŋpi kte.**

3. **Šúŋkawakȟáŋ etáŋ wičhúŋkauŋspepi kte.**

4. **Heháŋl wičhúŋkastopi kte.**

5. **Uŋnúŋwaŋpi na heháŋl waúŋyutapi kte.**

6. **Owápȟe šakówiŋ kiŋháŋ Bob lekšítku kičhí houŋkhuwapi kte.**

7. **Lakȟáš thiwówaši ečhúŋk'uŋpi kte héčha!**

**10** Look at the list of activities that Bob and Lisa are going to do with their friends. When Bob and Lisa tell Lisa's mom, they talk about their activities using the "we" forms of the verbs. Can you change each of these verbs to the "they" form, like the model? Then, write the dictionary form of each one.

| We form | They form | Dictionary form |
|---|---|---|
| 1. uŋnúŋwaŋpi | nuŋwáŋpi | nuŋwÁŋ |
| 2. uŋyáŋpi | _____ | _____ |
| 3. wičhúŋkauŋspepi | _____ | _____ |
| 4. wičhúŋkastopi | _____ | _____ |
| 5. waúŋyutapi | _____ | _____ |
| 6. houŋkhuwapi | _____ | _____ |
| 7. waŋyáŋg uŋyáŋkapi | _____ | _____ |
| 8. thiwówaši ečhúŋk'uŋpi | _____ | _____ |

**11** Let's look back at Bob's conversation with Tȟašúŋke-ska. For each of the dictionary forms below, find the "we" form that is used in the conversation. Write it in the blank, like the model.

| | | |
|---|---|---|
| khuté | ---> | uŋkhútepi |
| máni | | _____ |
| éthi | | _____ |
| wótA | | _____ |
| í | | _____ |
| iyáyA | | _____ |

**12** **a** How do we talk about the order of activities? Read through what Bob is telling Kimi and Lisa that they will do at the ranch, and then number the pictures in the order that they are going to happen.

**Toháŋl pteyúha othí ektá uŋyáŋpi kiŋháŋ, tȟokáheya šúŋkawakȟáŋ kiŋ wówičhuŋk'upi kte. Heháŋl uŋnúŋwaŋpi kte. Íŋska! Uŋnúŋwaŋpi kte itȟókab šuŋk'ákaŋuŋyaŋkapi kte. Heháŋl waúŋyutapi kte. Ehákeȟčiŋ wakší-uŋyužažapi kte.**

_____     _____     _____     1._____     _____

**b** Bob, Kimi, and Lisa are talking about what they will do on Sunday. Can you finish their conversation? Use words to show the order of activities. Look back at what Bob says in 12a if you need help.

1. _____ takúku uŋyútapi kte.

2. _____ tȟab'úŋškatapi kte.

3. _____ mnikápȟopapi opȟéuŋtȟuŋpi kta čha mas'óphiye-ta uŋyáŋpi kte.

4. _____ toháŋl waúŋtukȟapi kiŋháŋ, wičhítenaškaŋškaŋ waŋyáŋg uŋyáŋkapi kte.

# 13 It's your turn to plan an ideal day with some of your classmates!

**a** Work with a partner. You have a list of possible activities to choose from below. Talk to your partner to decide which activities the two of you will do, and in what order you will do them. You can choose to do only 4 things. On scratch paper, make a list of your choices, in order.

Here are your choices, in dictionary form: **nuŋwÁŋ, šuŋk'ákaŋyaŋkA, wótA, tȟabškátA, hokhúwa, wakhúl yÁ, wayáwa, lol'íȟ'aŋ, itówapi owá, kšú, wačhí, wičhítenaškaŋškaŋ waŋyáŋg yaŋkÁ, šiyótȟaŋka yažó, mas'óphiye-ta yÁ**

1st person: **Tȟokáheya šuŋk'ákaŋuŋyaŋka héči?**
2nd person: **Hiyá, šuŋk'ákaŋuŋyaŋkiŋ kte šni! Éeye tȟab'úŋškata héči.**
1st person: **Oháŋ, tȟab'úŋškatiŋ kte! Heháŋl houŋkhuwa kte!**
2nd person: **Oháŋ! Heháŋl uŋnúŋwiŋ kte!**
1st person: **Héčhetu! Ehákeȟčiŋ waúŋyutiŋ kte!**

**b** Now write sentences so that you can tell the rest of the class what you and your partner are going to do. Remember, to tell someone else, you need to switch from the "you-and-I" form to the "we" form!

*Tȟokáheya tȟab'úŋškatapi kte. Heháŋl šuŋk'ákaŋuŋyaŋkapi kte. Heháŋl waúŋyutapi kte. Ehákeȟčiŋ uŋnúŋwaŋpi kte.*

**č** Are your classmates going to do the same things you are? Ask two other people what they are going to do. Make notes about their choices in the chart.

**Táku tókȟanuŋpi kta he?**

**Tȟokáheya houŋkhuwapi kte. Heháŋl uŋnúŋwaŋpi kte. Ehákeȟčiŋ waúŋyutapi kte.**

| | Čhažé: _____ | Čhažé: _____ |
|---|---|---|
| **Tȟokáheya** | _____ | _____ |
| **Heháŋl** | _____ | _____ |
| **Heháŋl** | _____ | _____ |
| **Ehákeȟčiŋ** | _____ | _____ |

**13** **e** Now write sentences about what you found out, like the model.
What are your classmates going to do?

> Tȟokáheya Susie Justin kičhí tȟabškátapi kte. Heháŋl šuŋk'ákaŋyaŋkapi kte. Heháŋl wótapi kte. Ehákeȟčiŋ nuŋwáŋpi kte.

**14** What is happening to Bob now? First, look at the pictures. Then read through this part of the story. Can you match the pictures with what the story says? Write the number of each picture in the box of the matching phrase or sentence.

<u>3.</u> **Čhetȟípi šni, ičhíŋ owékinaháŋš tȟóka kiŋ waŋwíčhayaŋkapi kte.**

__ **Bob líla watúkȟa čha haŋp'íkčeka kiŋ glušlóke.**

__ **Tȟaté Wiŋ húŋku kiŋ hupáwaheyuŋpi kiŋ etáŋhaŋ wasná eyá ičú.**

__ **Thiwáhe kiŋ wówičhak'u kta čha ičú.**

__ **Na ištíŋme.**

__ **Oyáte kiŋ wakpá-aglágla ománipi.**

__ **Heháŋl iyúha šináhiŋšma akáŋlkaŋl ištíŋmapi.**

__ **Ȟtayétu eháŋl éthipi.**

**15** Look at coyote's questions and circle the answer that you think is true.

> **Bob thiyáta glí kta he? Tókhel ilúkčaŋ so?**

Háŋ     Hiyá.

> **Haŋp'íkčeka wakȟáŋ kiŋ ilágyiŋ kta he?**

Háŋ     Hiyá.

**1** Skim through this part of the story. Does Bob get home?

**Háŋ.  Hiyá.**

> Bob tȟoká kiktá. Uŋmá kiŋ héčhena ištíŋmape ló.

> Wáŋ! Líla čhuwí mastáke ičhíŋ makȟá kiŋ líla sutá. Tuwéni naháŋȟčiŋ kiktá šni. Uŋgnáš wakpála-ta mníŋ kte. Haŋp'íkčeka kiŋ tuktél míčiyaŋka he?

> Waŋná Bob thiyáta khí yeló. Oyáte kiŋ kiktá áyapi.

> Bob tókhi iyáya he?

> Máni iyáya s'eléčheča.

> Wakpála aglágla olé mníŋ kte.

> Bob iyéwaya owákihi šni.

> Thiyáta khiglé séče. Lisa íŋš-eyá léčhel tókȟaŋ'aŋ čha wéksuye. Uŋkíš takómni akhé iglág uŋkíyayapi kte héčha. Ičhíŋ kaíyuzeya uŋyáŋpi kte.

**2** Read through the story more carefully and then answer the questions below.

**a** Tuwá tȟoká kiktá he?
1) Míla Kič'úŋ.
2) Bob.
3) Tȟašúŋke-Ská.

**č** Bob haŋp'íkčeka kiŋ oháŋ yuŋkȟáŋ táku akhípȟa he?
1) Bob thiyáta khí.
2) Bob Matȟó Pahá-ta í.
3) Bob ištíŋme.

**b** Bob tókhiya iyáya he?
1) Čhaŋmáhel-ta iyáye.
2) Obláye-ta iyáye.
3) Wakpála-ta iyáye.

**e** Oyáte kiŋ táku tókȟuŋpi kta he?
1) Iglág iyáyapi kte.
2) Wótapi kte.
3) Tȟáȟča-khuwápi kte.

**3** Skim through the next part of the dialogue, between Tȟašúŋke-Ska and Míla Kič'úŋ. Are they talking to Bob and Lisa or about Bob and Lisa?

Circle the correct answer:     **To** Bob and Lisa.          **About** Bob and Lisa.

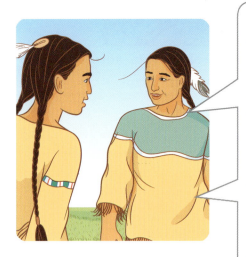

Míla Kič'úŋ: **Bob kȟoúŋkipȟapi he?**

Tȟašúŋke-Ská:  Hiyá, Bob kȟoúŋkipȟapi šni.
Bob waštéuŋlakapi na nakúŋ uŋyúonihaŋpi.

Míla Kič'úŋ: **Bob tuktétaŋhaŋ he?**

Tȟašúŋke-Ská: Tuktétaŋhaŋ ka héči. Lisa tuktétaŋhaŋ kiŋ hé íŋš-eyá
hetáŋhaŋ séče. Lakȟól'iyapi éyaš wóiȟake s'e  iglúzapi.

Míla Kič'úŋ: **Bob é na Lisa uŋkíye ób uŋk'úŋpi kta he?**

Tȟašúŋke-Ská: Uŋkíye ób uŋk'úŋpi kte šni. Akhéšna thiyáta khiglápi kte
iyéčheča. Thiyáta yaŋkápi šni háŋtaŋš thiwáhe kiŋ iyókišičapi kte.

Míla Kič'úŋ: **Bob é na Lisa akhé waŋúŋyaŋkapi čhíŋpi kta he?**

Tȟašúŋke-Ská: Háŋ, čhíŋpi kta kéčhaŋmi. Táku uŋspéwičhuŋkhiyapi kte
kiŋ hená óta yeló.

**4** Now read through the dialogue between Míla Kič'úŋ and Tȟašúŋke-Ská. Then write out answers to the
questions. Try to use complete sentences in your answers.

**a** Bob oyáte kiŋ kȟowíčhakipȟa he?          _____

**b** Bob oyáte kiŋ waštéwičhalaka he?          _____

**č** Bob oyáte kiŋ wičháyuonihaŋ he?          _____

**e** Bob é na Lisa oyáte kiŋ ób éna úŋpi kta he?          _____

**g** Oyáte kiŋ Bob é na Lisa akhé waŋwíčhayaŋkapi kta he?          _____

## 5 Abléza po!

You already know how to say that "we" do something: **Šúŋka waŋ waŋúŋyaŋkapi**. -- We saw a dog.

Now let's look at another meaning for verbs with the personal affix "**uŋ(k)**." Study the sentences and pictures below. What is the second meaning for the "**uŋ(k)**" affix in these sentences?

Circle it: **US   HIM   THEM**

Hokšíla kiŋ waŋúŋyaŋkapi.

Wičhíŋčala kiŋ wówapi kiŋ lé uŋk'úpi.

Wičháša kiŋ wóuŋk'upi.

**6** Summer and Tȟašína are writing text messages to tell their mothers what is happening to them at school. "Bob gave us a hug," they tell her. What else do they say? Match the sentences on the left with the pictures on the right.

1. Bob pȟóskil uŋyúzapi.
2. Hokšíla waŋ naúŋȟtakapi.
3. Waúŋspewičhakhiye kiŋ napé uŋyúzapi.
4. Wičhíŋčala kiŋ uŋkápȟapi.
5. James yuš'íŋyeuŋyaŋpi.
6. Hokšíla waŋ uŋkáiȟat'api.
7. Lisa wówapi eyá uŋk'úpi.
8. Kimi íuŋkiputȟakapi.
9. Mike waŋúŋyaŋkapi.
10. Matȟó waŋyáŋg uŋhípi.

**7** Pretend you are on the set of a movie! Three students will get up. One will mime doing something to the other two. The two students will report to the class on "what's being done to us", like the model.

Suggestions for activities you can do: **pȟóskil yúzA, k'ú, waŋyáŋkA, yuš'íŋyeyA, íiputȟakA, waŋyáŋg hí, ačháŋzekA, aíȟat'A, theȟíla, napé yúzA, naȟtákA, wók'u, mas'ápȟA.**

Denise wówapi waŋ uŋk'úpi.

Waŋná Bob táku akhípȟa he?

Lisa: **Tȟéhaŋ yaglí šni! Nihíŋčiyemayaye!**

Bob: **Yámni-čhaŋ Lakȟóta oyáte kiŋ ób omáwani. Áta khilí!**

**8** Skim through the dialogue below.
What are the children going to buy at the store?
**Circle the correct picture.**

Kimi and James: **Aŋpétu átaya waŋúŋniyaŋkapi šni. Mas'áuŋničipȟapi éyaš tuwéni uŋkáyuptapi šni.**

Bob and Lisa: Uŋčí tȟa-čháŋthipi kiŋ ektá uŋkípi. Ečháŋni mas'áuŋničipȟapi kte, éyaš uŋkókihipi šni.

Kimi and James: **Kitáŋla uŋkáničhaŋzekapi. Mas'óphiye-ta uŋyáŋpi kte kiŋ yéksuyapi šni he?**

Bob: Uŋkáčhaŋzekapi šni yo.

Lisa: **Toháŋl mas'óphiye-ta uŋkípi kiŋháŋ mázaska etáŋ uŋníč'upi kte, héčhel mnikápȟopapi etáŋ opȟéyatȟuŋpi kte.**

James: **Áta nikhílipe ló. Ho po, uŋyáŋpi kte.**

**9** Read the dialogue again and circle the correct answer to these questions.

**a** Bob glí yuŋkȟáŋ Lisa tóktuka he?
- Nihíŋčiye.
- Iyókiphi.
- Ačháŋzeke.

**b** Bob Lakȟóta oyáte kiŋ ób toháŋyaŋ ománi he?
- Aŋpétu óta.
- Waníyetu tóna.
- Aŋpétu tóna.

**č** Lisa é na Bob henáos Kimi é na James awíčhayuptapi šni. Tákuwe?
- Ičhíŋ Lisa kȟúŋšitku tȟa-čháŋthipi kiŋ ektá ípi.
- Ičhíŋ Lisa kȟúŋšitku tȟa-čháŋthipi kiŋ iléyapi.
- Ičhíŋ Lisa kȟúŋšitku tȟa-čháŋthipi kiŋ opȟétȟuŋpi.

**e** Kimi é na James tókhiya yápi čhíŋpi he?
- Otȟúŋwahe-ta yápi čhíŋpi.
- Mas'óphiye-ta yápi čhíŋpi.
- Wígli oínažiŋ-ta yápi čhíŋpi.

**g** Bob é na Lisa henáos Kimi é na James táku wičhák'upi kta he?
- Mnikápȟopapi etáŋ.
- Čháŋthipi waŋží.
- Mázaska etáŋ.

**10** # Abléza po!

Let's look at a new pattern! You already know how to say that **he** or **she** did something to you. Look at these examples:

**Waŋníyaŋke.  Theníȟila.  Yuš'íŋyeniye.**

You also know how to say that **we** did something (to him or her). Look at these examples:

**Waŋúŋyaŋkapi.  Theúŋȟilapi.  Yuš'íŋyeuŋyaŋpi.**

Now, let's put these two patterns together, to say that "**WE** do something to **YOU**." Look at the following examples. Which affix comes first? The one for "**we**" or the one for "**you**?"

**Waŋúŋniyaŋkapi.  Theúŋniȟilapi.  Yuš'íŋyeuŋniyaŋpi.**

Write your answer here: _____

**11** Each of the sentences below talks about something that WE did to HIM or HER. Can you change these sentences to talk about what WE did to YOU?

| | | | |
|---|---|---|---|
| 1. Yuš'íŋyeuŋyaŋpi. | 1. Yuš'íŋyeuŋniyaŋpi. | 6. Waštéuŋlakapi. | 6. _____ |
| 2. Uŋyúonihaŋpi. | 2. _____ | 7. Anáuŋǧoptaŋpi. | 7. _____ |
| 3. Napé uŋyúzapi. | 3. _____ | 8. Naúŋȟ'uŋpi. | 8. _____ |
| 4. Uŋyúȟičapi. | 4. _____ | 9. Uŋyáȟtakapi. | 9. _____ |
| 5. Slol'úŋyaŋpi. | 5. _____ | 10. Naúŋȟtakapi. | 10. _____ |

## 12 Abléza po!

You already know that sometimes **uŋ(k)** does not go in the same place that other personal affixes do. Study the following examples. Circle each one in which **uŋ(k)** and **ni** are separated.

**Waŋúŋniyaŋkapi.** (We saw you.)      **Theúŋniñilapi.** (We love you.)

**Yuš'íŋyeuŋniyaŋpi.** (We scared you.)      **Uŋkáničhaŋzekapi.** (We are angry with you.)

**Uŋkónilepi.** (We looked for you.)      **Uŋkáiniñat'api.** (We laughed at you.)

**13** Kimi is having a lot of trouble with her homework! She has some sentences that talk about what "we" are doing to him or her. She wants to change the sentences to say that "We are doing something to you." Can you help her?

First, match the "we" form with its dictionary form. Draw lines to match.
Then, rewrite the sentences for Kimi, like the model below.

| | | |
|---|---|---|
| Uŋkáčhaŋzekapi. | apȟá | _____ |
| Uŋkápȟapi. | oyákA | _____ |
| Uŋkáyuptapi. | ačháŋzekA | *Uŋkáničhaŋzekapi.* |
| Uŋkápsičapi. | ayúta | _____ |
| Uŋkóyakapi. | oyúspA | _____ |
| Uŋkáyutapi. | apsíčA | _____ |
| Uŋkóyuspapi. | ayúptA | _____ |

**14** You already learned about how the "**k**" sound changes when we add "**ni**," but Kimi is just learning about how to make this change. Can you help her? She is trying to figure out how to write some different verbs, but the teacher marked some of her answers wrong! Can you help her by correcting the change from **k** to **č** where it is needed?

Help Kimi with the correct answers here!

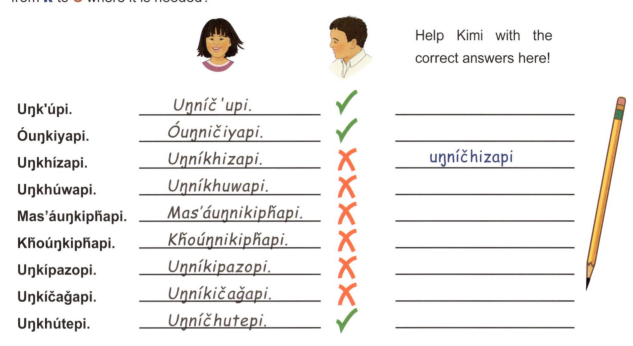

| | | | |
|---|---|---|---|
| Uŋk'úpi. | Uŋníč'upi. | ✓ | |
| Óuŋkiyapi. | Óuŋničiyapi. | ✓ | |
| Uŋkhízapi. | Uŋníkhizapi. | ✗ | uŋníčhizapi |
| Uŋkhúwapi. | Uŋníkhuwapi. | ✗ | |
| Mas'áuŋkipȟapi. | Mas'áuŋnikipȟapi. | ✗ | |
| Kȟoúŋkipȟapi. | Kȟoúŋnikipȟapi. | ✗ | |
| Uŋkípazopi. | Uŋníkipazopi. | ✗ | |
| Uŋkíčağapi. | Uŋníkičağapi. | ✗ | |
| Uŋkhútepi. | Uŋníčhutepi. | ✓ | |

**15 a** Are Lisa and Kimi talking to one person, or to more than one person? How do you know? For each dialogue, draw stick figures to show how many people Lisa and Kimi are talking to.

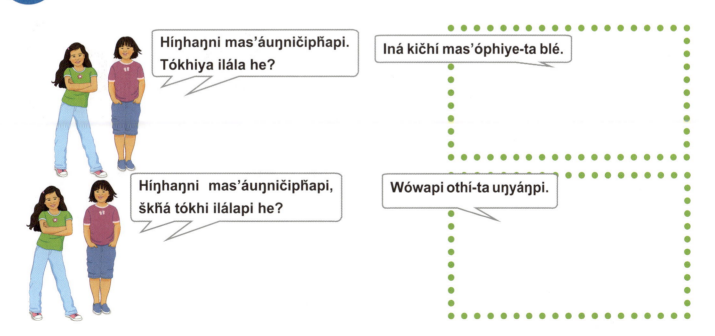

Híŋhaŋni mas'áuŋničipȟapi. Tókhiya ilála he?

Iná kičhí mas'óphiye-ta blé.

Híŋhaŋni mas'áuŋničipȟapi, škȟá tókhi ilálapi he?

Wówapi othí-ta uŋyáŋpi.

**b** Which of the two verbs in each question helped you to figure out how many people Lisa and Kimi are talking to? Circle them.

**16** You are planning a weekend get together outdoors. First, find a partner. Then, get in two lines of partners, facing each other.

**Invite the partners across from you. They will tell you what they will give you. Make plans to call each other to finalize plans, like the model.**

> Okóihaŋke kiŋháŋ čhúŋšoke-ta uŋyáŋpi kte. Níš-eyá lápi kta he?

> Čhiŋtók! Uŋyáŋpi kte. Mnikápȟopapi etáŋ uŋníč'upi kte!

> Wašté! Aŋpétu Záptaŋ kiŋháŋ mas'áuŋničipȟapi kte!

**17** Sometimes in school, people will try to bully you. Let's practice responding to this kind of bad behavior in Lakota! **Find a partner, and get in two lines of partners like the previous exercise.** One group will _pretend_ to be the bullies. The other group will answer them back. You have several suggestions of what a bully might say to you and your friends, and several suggestions for how to answer.

Pretend bullies can say these things:

Uŋkánipȟapi kte!

Naúŋniȟtakapi kte!

To answer the bullies, we can say:

Wóuŋničiyakapi kte šni!

Uŋkóniyakapi kte!

Uŋkóničhuwapi kte!

Uŋníyaȟtakapi kte!

Anáuŋniǧoptaŋpi kte šni!

Uŋníčhizapi kte šni!

Uŋkáiniȟat'api kte!

Kȟóuŋničipȟapi šni!

**18** **a** You and your class have gotten funding to go and visit one of the following (your choice!): the Cree, living in Canada, the Maori, living in New Zealand, or the Hawaiians. Although you will write to them in English, you also want to write a letter in Lakota, to tell them when you will see them, what you will bring them, and add something about how you feel about them: Do you have respect for them? **Look at the model sentences, and then write three or four of your own sentences to introduce yourself to the people you will visit.**

Mitákuyepi,

čhaŋtéwašteya napéuŋniyuzapi.
Blokéhaŋ iyúškiŋyaŋ waŋúŋniyaŋkapi.
Ečháŋni akhé waŋníyaŋg uŋyáŋpi kte.

_____

_____

_____

_____

_____

Tókša waŋúŋniyaŋkapi kte.
_____ na _____
(čhažé)           (čhažé)

You can make sentences with these verbs, or others that you think of: **yuónihaŋ, iyúŋǧA, waštélakA, mas'ákipȟA, k'ú, okíyakA, kipázo**. Here are some new verbs you can try: **kaú** (bring something to someone), **ikimna** (admire). If you don't have enough room on this page, write your letter on scratch paper.

**b** When you have finished, exchange your letter with a partner. You want the letters you send to be really good, so help your partner out by correcting any spelling or grammar mistakes!

> Waŋná Bob é na Lisa táku čha akhípȟapi he?
> Oyúblaye íyokhihe kiŋ ektá éslol'uŋyaŋpi kte.

**1** Skim through the dialogue on this page, read the question, and circle the best answer.

**Lisa tákuwe čha wáŋčag iyúŋka he?**

Wakȟáŋheža kiŋ mas'óphiye-ta ípi.
Heháŋl iyúha thiyáta khípi. Lisa líla watúkȟa čha wáŋčag iyúŋke....

Waŋná híŋhaŋni. Lisa kiktá kte héčha.

Lisa, kiktá ye! Owóhiŋsko yaȟpáya-he!

Oháŋ, Iná!

Haŋp'íkčeka kiŋ owáhiŋ kte!
Líla waštéšte!

**2** Let's see what's happening now in our story! Skim through the dialogue below, read the question, and circle the correct answer.

**Lakȟól oyáte kiŋ aŋpétu kiŋ lé táku tókȟuŋpi kta he?**

Tȟaté Wiŋ: **Má, akhé yaglí so! Lekší akhé yaglí kta kéye. Oyáte kiŋ thiíkčeya kiŋ pawóslaslal iyékiyapi kte. Ówičhuŋkiya héči?**

Lisa: **Takómni ówičhuŋkiyiŋ kte! Tȟokéya táku tókȟuŋk'uŋ kta he?**

Tȟaté Wiŋ: **Iná uŋkíyuŋǧiŋ kte. Thikáǧapi wóphike kštó.**

Tȟaté Wiŋ: **Iná, Lisa kičhí thiúŋkaǧapi kta uŋčhíŋpi, éyaš uŋkúŋspepi šni.**

Iná: **Čhičípazopi kte. Taŋyáŋ waŋyáŋg nážiŋ pe!**

**3** Read through the dialogue on both pages again, and then choose the best answer for each of the questions below.

**1** **Tuwá Lisa yuȟíča he?**
a) Tȟuŋwíŋču.　b) Húŋku.　č) Čhuwéku.

**2** **Lisa haŋp'íkčeka wakȟáŋ kiŋ ohán yuŋkȟáŋ táku akhípȟa he?**
a) Mas'óphiye-ta í.
b) Lakȟól wičhóthi-ta í.
č) Owáyawa-ta í.

**3** **Tȟaté Wiŋ thiíkčeya kiŋ tókheškhe pawóslal iyéyapi héči tuwá iyúŋǧa he?**
a) Lekšítku　b) Húŋku.　č) Kȟúŋšitku.

**4** **Tȟaté Wiŋ húŋku kiŋ táku uŋspéwičhakhiyiŋ kta he?**
a) Tȟáȟča-khutépi uŋspéwičhakhiyiŋ kte.
b) Haŋp'íkčeka káǧapi uŋspéwičhakhiyiŋ kte.
č) Thikáǧapi uŋspéwičhakhiyiŋ kte.

**4** Tȟaté-wiŋ's mother told Lisa all the parts of a tipi, and she made this drawing. Study it carefully, and then close your book. Your teacher will give you a blank picture to label. Work with a partner, and fill in as many as you can. Once you have finished, check back in the book if there are some you couldn't remember.

Wičhóiye kiŋ lená kiksúya ye! Wawóyakiya čháŋna wičhóiye kiŋ lená núŋ kte.

Oháŋ!

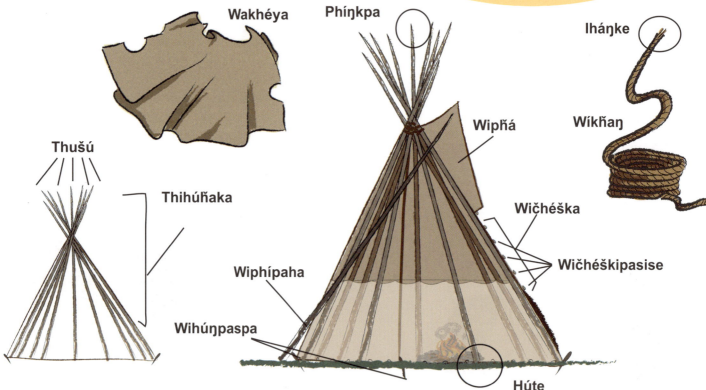

Wakhéya

Phíŋkpa

Iháŋke

Wipȟá

Wíkȟaŋ

Thušú

Thihúȟaka

Wičhéška

Wičhéškipasise

Wiphípaha

Wihúŋpaspa

Húte

**5 a** Stand in a circle. Your teacher will give each of you a card with one of the parts of the tipi on it. Take turns asking your classmates to pass you what they are holding, like the model.

**Wakhéya kiŋ hiyúmakhiya ye! (female student)**

**Oháŋ, wakhéya kiŋ hiyúčhičhiyiŋ kte! (female or male)**

**b** Now your teacher will put the cards on a table. Ask one of your classmates to get one of the tipi parts for you.

**Wakhéya kiŋ imákiču we! (female student)**

**Oháŋ, wakhéya kiŋ ičhíčiču kte! (female or male)**

**č** Next your teacher will tape all of the cards up on the wall. Ask one of your classmates to take something down for you.

Model: **Wakhéya kiŋ makíyuȟpa yo. (male student)**

**Oháŋ, wakhéya kiŋ čhičíyuȟpiŋ kte.**

**5e** Now, on scratch paper, write some sentences about what your classmates did for someone, like the models. Write at least 6 sentences, two with each verb.

> Susie Bettie wakhéya kiŋ hiyúkhiye.
> Nancy Peter wakhéya kiŋ ikíču.
> David John wakhéya kiŋ kiyúȟpe.

**6** Lisa knows her directions in Lakota, as you can see from her conversation with Ťȟaté-wiŋ's mother. How about you? Can you label the directions on this map? Write the name of each of the directions on the line provided.

Ťȟatúye tópa kiŋ Lakȟól'iya čhažéyatapi uŋníspe he?

Oháŋ!

Wašté!

**7  Abléza po!**

You know that **wazíyata** is north. But how do we talk about going towards the north, or coming from the north? We need to add some endings to the word! Look at the pictures and read the sentences below. Then circle the correct answers to the questions.

wazíyata

wazíyata

**Wazíyatakiya ománi.**          **Wazíyataŋhaŋ hí.**

Which of the endings means "**from the** ...."?    -takiya    -taŋhaŋ
Which of the endings means "**towards the** ...."?    -takiya    -taŋhaŋ

**8 a** Leaders have come from all over to meet at Lower Brule to discuss treaty rights. The Crow (**Kȟaŋǧí Oyáte**) [from the west], the Pawnee (**Sčíli Oyáte**) [from the south], the Yanktonai-Dakota (**Iháŋktȟuŋwaŋna Oyáte**) [from the east], the Cree (**Maštíŋča Oyáte**) [from the north].Can you write sentences to talk about which direction each tribe came from, like the model?

*Maštíŋča Oyáte itȟáŋčhaŋ kiŋ wazíyataŋhaŋ hípi.*

wazíyata

**b** Now the leaders are returning home. Can you write about which direction each group will go, like the model?

*Maštíŋča Oyáte kiŋ wazíyatakiya glápi.*

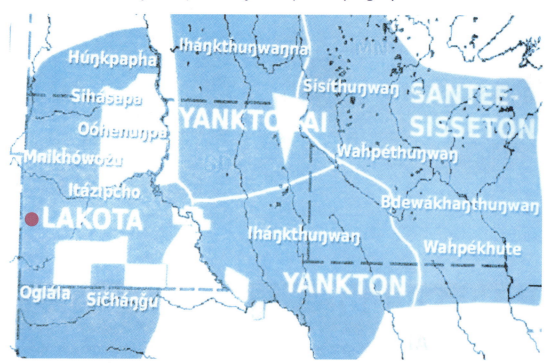

**9 a** Everyone stand in the middle of the room. Your teacher will show you which way is north, south, east and west in your classroom.  When your teacher tells you to, walk in the direction he or she tells you, while saying what you are doing.

**Wazíyatakiya yá yo!**

**Oháŋ, wazíyatakiya mníŋ kte!**

**b** Now, when your teacher calls your name, come BACK to where she or he is.  Then say what you did, like the model:

**Wazíyataŋhaŋ kú wo.**

**Oháŋ, wazíyataŋhaŋ wakú kte.**

**10** Lisa made notes and little drawings as Ťaté-wiŋ's mother told her how to put up a tipi. Can you figure out how to do it from the notes she made? Look at the vocabulary list below, of all the things you need to do to set up a tipi. Then, find and circle one example of each action in the tipi set-up directions on pages 72 and 73.

**pawóslal égle**

**yubláŋ égnaka**

**yut'íŋst'iŋza**

**yukážal égle**

**yubláya éuŋpa**

**čhokáŋgnagya éuŋpa**

**óštaŋ**

**ipásisa**

**aóhomniyaŋ máni**

**aópemni**

**okátaŋ**

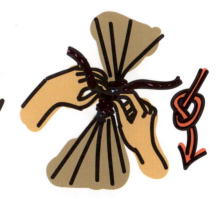

**akhíčaškA**

**1**

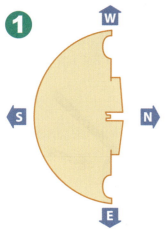

Wakhéya kiŋ yubláya éuŋpa pe. Wipĥá kiŋ wazíyatakiya épazo éuŋpa pe.

**2**

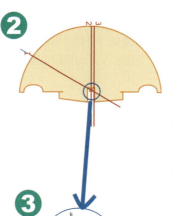

**3**

Thušú núŋm ičúpi na wakhéya kiŋ akáŋl čhokáŋgnagya éuŋpa pe. Thušú húte kiŋ itókaǧataŋhaŋ éuŋpapi na thušú phíŋkpa kiŋ wazíyatakiya épazo éuŋpa pe.

Akhé thušú waŋží ičúpi na núŋpa k'uŋ henáyos glakíŋyaŋ akáŋl éuŋpa pe. Thušú húte kiŋ thiyópa-ikhíyela éuŋpa pe. Thušú húte kiŋ kitáŋla wakhéya opápuŋ kiŋ iyópteya éuŋpa pe.

Wíkĥaŋ háŋska waŋží ičúpi na iháŋke kiŋ thušú yámni kiŋ tónakiya iyúwi na yuósiŋyaŋ akhíčaška pe.

**4**

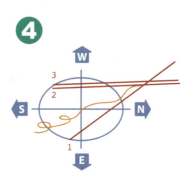

Thušú yámni k'uŋ hená ičúpi na thiíkčeya kiŋ tuktél híŋ kta héči kákhiya éuŋpa pe.

**5**

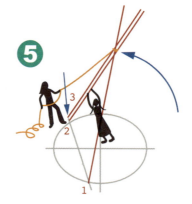

Thušú yámni kiŋ waŋná pawóslal égle pe.

**6**

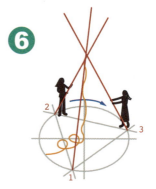

Thušú ičíyamni kiŋ ičúpi na wazíyatakiya yukážal égle pe. Lé ithíčhičaske eyápi.

**7**

Thušú yámni ičúpi na wazíyataŋhaŋ okhížata kiŋ ogná pawóslal égle pe.

**8**

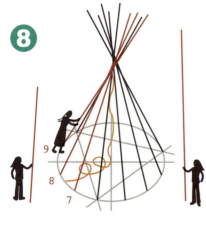

Akhé thušú yámni ičúpi na itókaǧataŋhaŋ okhížata kiŋ ogná pawóslal égle pe.

**9**

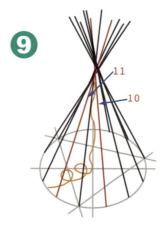

Akhé thušú núŋm ičúpi na wiyóĥpeyataŋhaŋ okhížata kiŋ ogná pawóslal égle pe.

**10**

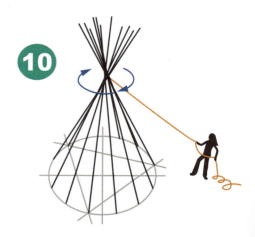

Wíkĥaŋ kiŋ ičúpi na thihúŋaka kiŋ aóhomniyaŋ wí hiyáye kiŋ iyéčhel máni pe. Tópa akhígle aóhomniyaŋ máni pe. Wíkĥaŋ kiŋ yut'íŋst'iŋza pe.

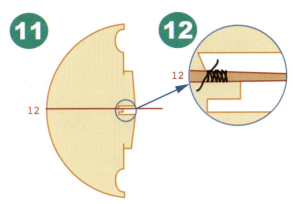

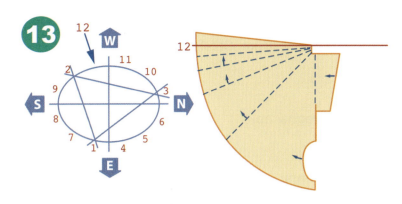

Thušú eháke kiŋ ičúpi na wakhéyaska kiŋ akáŋl éuŋpa pe. Thušú eháke kiŋ lé wíyapaȟiče eyápi. Wakhéya kiŋ thušú kiŋ él akhíčaška pe.

Wakhéya kiŋ thušú eháke kiŋ átaya aópemni pe.

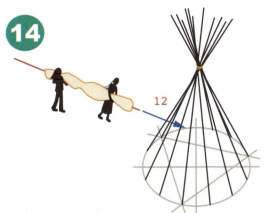

Waŋná thušú kiŋ wakhéya kiŋ óǧeya pawóslal égle pe.

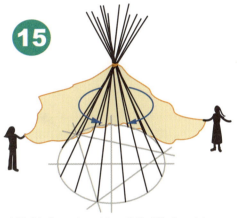

Wakhéyaska kiŋ thihúȟaka kiŋ aókawiŋȟ yubláya égnaka pe.

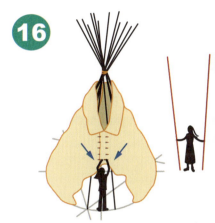

Wičhéškipasise kiŋ ičúpi na úŋ wičhéška kiŋ ipásisa pe.

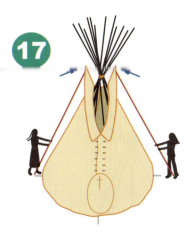

Wiphípaha kiŋ henáyos ičúpi na wipȟá phíŋkpa kiŋ ečhékče óštaŋ pe.

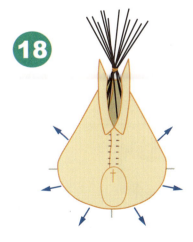

Thušú kiŋ thimáhetaŋhaŋ patȟáŋktȟaŋkal égle pe. Héčhel wakhéyaska kiŋ yubláȟ éyagnakapi kte.

Wihúta kiŋ ohómniyaŋ wihúŋpaspa kiŋ uŋ sutáya yuzígzil okátaŋ pe. Thihúȟaka kiŋ wíkȟaŋ kiŋ úŋ thimáhel yutítaŋ okátaŋ pe.

**11** Which of these activities go with which things? Do you remember? Draw lines from each activity to the correct picture. Careful! Some pictures will be used more than once, but use each picture at least once.

yubláŋ éyagnakapi

yubláya éuŋpa

čhokáŋgnagya éuŋpa

pawóslal égle

yukážal égle

pawáŋkal égle

akhíčaškA

yubláŋ égnaka

ipásisa

okátaŋ

óštaŋ

aópemni

aóhomniyaŋ máni

**12** Setting up a tipi can be complicated! Lisa is trying to make some notes, but she is forgetting the steps. Can you help her? For each picture below, circle the correct choice for what comes next. If you're not sure, look back at the tipi setup directions on pages 72 and 73.

**1**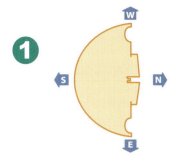

a. Thušú núŋm ičúpi na wakhéya kiŋ akáŋl čhokáŋgnagya éuŋpa pe.

b. Thušú eháke kiŋ ičúpi na wakhéya kiŋ akáŋl éuŋpa pe.

**2**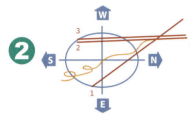

a. Wíkȟaŋ háŋska waŋží ičúpi na thušú yámni kiŋ yuósiŋyaŋ akhíčaška pe.

b. Thušú yámni kiŋ waŋná pawóslal égle pe.

**3**

a. Akhé thušú yámni ičúpi na itókaǧataŋhaŋ okhížata kiŋ ogná pawóslal égle pe.

b. Wakhéya kiŋ yubláya éuŋpa pe, wipȟá kiŋ wazíyatakiya épazo.

**4**

a. Wakhéya kiŋ thušú kiŋ opémni pe.

b. Wakhéyaska kiŋ thihúȟaka kiŋ aókawiŋȟ yubláya égnaka pe.

**5**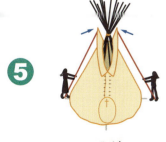

a. Thušú kiŋ thimáhetaŋhaŋ patȟáŋktȟaŋkal égle pe.

b. Wakhéya kiŋ thušú kiŋ él akhíčaška pe.

**6**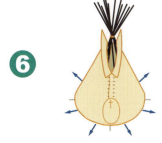

a. Thušú kiŋ thimáhetaŋhaŋ patȟáŋktȟaŋkal égle pe.

b. Wihúta kiŋ ohómniyaŋ wihúŋpaspa kiŋ uŋ sutáya yuzígzil okátaŋ pe.

**13** Let's play a game! Get into two teams. One person from each team goes up to the board. The teacher will show the students at the board one of the activities that you do to put up a tipi. The teacher will show the students at the board a picture of one of the activities done when setting up a tipi. The team that guesses the most correctly first wins!

> Waŋná Lisa thiíkčeya pawóslal iyéyapi uŋspé. Kiksúyiŋ kta he? Níš tók? Takúku uŋníspe he? Thiíkčeya pawóslal iyéyapi uŋníspe he?

**14** Let's answer the coyote's question! Which of these activities do you and your classmates know how to do? Ask three classmates and fill in the chart, circling the correct answer.

|                                         | Čhažé |       | Čhažé |       | Čhažé |       |
|-----------------------------------------|-------|-------|-------|-------|-------|-------|
|                                         | _____ | | _____ | | _____ | |
| Thiíkčeya iyéyapi uŋníspe he?           | Háŋ   | Hiyá. | Háŋ   | Hiyá. | Háŋ   | Hiyá. |
| Háŋpapȟečhuŋpi uŋníspe he?              | Háŋ   | Hiyá. | Háŋ   | Hiyá. | Háŋ   | Hiyá. |
| Šuŋk'ákaŋyaŋkapi uŋníspe he?            | Háŋ   | Hiyá. | Háŋ   | Hiyá. | Háŋ   | Hiyá. |
| Wakhúl yápi uŋníspe he?                 | Háŋ   | Hiyá. | Háŋ   | Hiyá. | Háŋ   | Hiyá. |
| Pȟežíȟota olépi uŋníspe he?             | Háŋ   | Hiyá. | Háŋ   | Hiyá. | Háŋ   | Hiyá. |
| Thíŋpsiŋla ok'ápi uŋníspe he?           | Háŋ   | Hiyá. | Háŋ   | Hiyá. | Háŋ   | Hiyá. |

**15**

> Wanásapi uŋníspe he? Na Bob íŋš uŋspé he? Uŋgnáš Lakȟóta kiŋ Bob uŋspékhiyapi kte! Oyúblaye íyokhihe kiŋ ektá éslol'uŋyaŋpi kte.

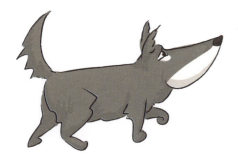

**1** Now that the tipis are up, everything else needs to be put away! But first the girls have to find everything! Skim through the dialogue below, and then match each object with its location.

W:  **Tuktél ptehíŋšma kiŋ yaŋká he?**

Isa:  **Ptehíŋšma kiŋ čháŋ isákhib yaŋké. Naháŋ tȟaŋpá mniógnake kiŋ lé tuktél háŋ he?**

W:  **Thiíkčeya kiŋ ilázata hé. Čhéǧa kiŋ héčhena wakpála kiŋ isákhib yaŋká he?**

Isa:  **Háŋ, naháŋ waléǧa kiŋ lé tuktél yaŋká he?**

W:  **Čhaŋáletka kiŋ etáŋhaŋ otké. Thibló tȟa-ítazipa kiŋ lé čháŋ kiŋ íčaŋyaŋ hé. Imákičú we!**

Isa:  **Oháŋ, ičhíčičú kte. Čhaŋwákšiča kiŋ waŋláka he?**

W:  **Ptehíŋšma kiŋ akáŋl hé šni he?**

Isa:  **Hiyá!**

W:  **Háš! Tuktél yaŋká he?**

**2** Circle the correct answer:
**Wičhíŋčala kiŋ táku čha iyéyapi šni he?**

## 3 Abléza po!

Like English, Lakota uses words to tell the position of things. Often, the shape of the thing will tell you what verb to use. Read the sentences below, and then write the verb next to the arrows.

Žaŋžáŋla kiŋ wáglutapi kiŋ akáŋl hé.

Čháŋ kiŋ makȟá akáŋl ȟpáye.

Wakšíča kiŋ owákšiyužaža kiŋ mahél yaŋké.

Pȟežíȟota kiŋ sáta waŋ etáŋhaŋ otké.

 _____
Vertical things with a narrow base (tree, bottle, but also a car).

 _____
Things that are hanging from something.

 _____
Long things that lie (rope, river, log, stretched rope).

 _____
Things that have a wide base (dish, blanket, coiled rope).

4 Kimi is describing her room to a friend she met on the Lakota language forum. She is trying to write all in Lakota, so she and her friend can practice, but she is not sure of her verbs! Can you help her? Finish the sentences using **ȟpáyA, yaŋkÁ, otkÁ,** or **hÁŋ**, depending on the object.

**a** Ipáhiŋ waŋ oyúŋke kiŋ akáŋl _____ .

**b** Čhuwígnaka waŋ haótkeye kiŋ mahél _____ .

**č** Owíŋža waŋ oyúŋke kiŋ akáŋl _____ .

**e** Tȟap'íčakȟape waŋ thiókaȟmi él _____ .

**g** Owíŋ kiŋ wíkȟaŋ kiŋ etáŋhaŋ _____ .

**ǧ** Hunáhomnipi kiŋ ožáŋžaŋglepi kiŋ itȟáŋkal _____ .

**h** Šiyótȟaŋka waŋ akáŋwowapi kiŋ akáŋl _____ .

**ȟ** Oákaŋke waŋ akáŋwowapi kiŋ itȟókab _____ .

**5** Now it's your turn! Where are the objects in the yard?

**a** Work in pairs and decide which one of you is "partner one" and which one is "partner two". Partner one looks at the image of a blue house and yard on page 141. Partner two looks at the image of a yellow house and yard on page 142. Then write sentences about where the things are, like the model. Don't show the picture or your sentences to your partner.

Igmú kiŋ čhaŋáletka waŋ akáŋl yaŋké.

**b** Now, work with your partner. Look at the image of the house and yard again. Don't look at your partner's picture! Listen to what s/he says about where the things are sitting, standing or lying in his/her picture. Then draw the things on the blank picture of the house that your teacher gives you (s/he will photo-copy it from page 145). When you have finished, compare your drawing to your partner's sentences.

**6** Your teacher will give each of you a picture. Stand in a circle with your classmates. When someone asks you, show your picture, and say what it is, like the model.

> Itówapi kiŋ makípazo we!

> Oháŋ! Kiŋyékhiyapi kiŋ wíkȟaŋ waŋ etáŋhaŋ otké.

**7** Now that the girls have found most everything, they have to put things away! Skim through this conversation, and circle the items that Lisa and Tȟaté-wiŋ actually do put away.

Tȟaté-wiŋ: **Waŋná takúku óta thimáhel éuŋgnakiŋ kte héčha.**

Lisa: Oháŋ, héčhuŋk'uŋ kte! Tȟokáheya táku tókȟuŋk'uŋ kta he?

Tȟaté-wiŋ: **Thibló tȟa-ítazipa kiŋ čháŋ kiŋ íčaŋyaŋ háŋ čha waŋláka he? Thimáhel wazíyataŋhaŋ égle ye.**

Lisa: Oháŋ, naháŋ ptehá waŋ kál yaŋké kiŋ tókhiya éwagnakiŋ kta he?

Tȟaté-wiŋ: **Čhatkúta égnaka ye.**

Lisa: Wáŋžu waŋ kál otké kiŋ tuktél otkéwayiŋ kta he?

Tȟaté-wiŋ: **Hé nakúŋ thimáhel wazíyataŋhaŋ otkéya ye.**

Lisa: Ká tȟaŋpá mniógnake kiŋ tuktél éwagle kta he?

Tȟaté-wiŋ: **Thimáhel itókaǧataŋhaŋ égle ye, thiyópa kiŋ isákhib. Naháŋ čhaŋkázuŋtapi waŋ kál íŋyaŋ kiŋ akáŋl yaŋká čha waŋláka he? Čhatkúta égnaka ye.**

Lisa: Oháŋ! Čhaŋtéwašteya óčhičiye kštó. Waŋná líla ímapuze láȟ.

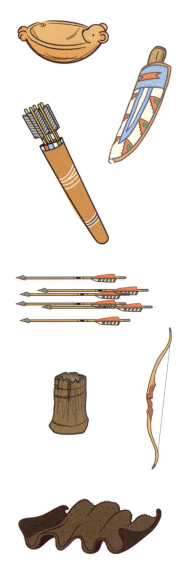

**8** Look at the interior of the tipi and read the dialogue again. Draw arrows to show where the girls put each of the items in the tipi.

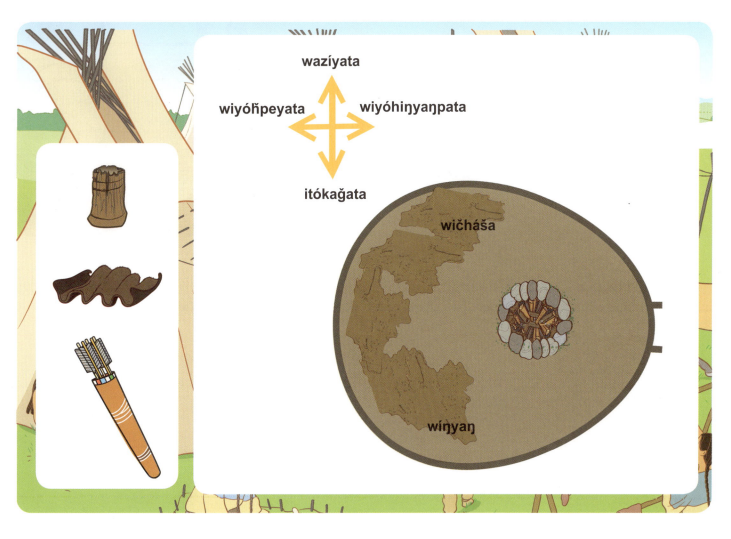

wazíyata

wiyóȟpeyata    wiyóhiŋyaŋpata

itókaǧata

wičháša

wíŋyaŋ

## 9 Abléza po!

Like English, when we put things away, we use words to show the position of the object. You already know the verbs to talk about things that sit, lie, stand and hang. Now match those verbs to the verbs for positioning things in Lakota.

| | |
|---|---|
| yaŋkÁ | égle |
| hÁŋ | éuŋpA |
| ȟpáyA | otkéyA |
| otkÁ | égnakA |

**10** Pretend you are moving into a new place with your family. Your mom, dad or grandma are telling you where to put things. Look at the objects, and decide which verbs they would use. Would you stand, sit, hang or lay the object? Draw a line from each object to a verb. You will use each verb more than once.

**11** Matȟó needs to find some verb forms in the dictionary. Can you help him? Use the dictionary to find the "I" and the "we" forms, then you can figure out the "you" and the "you and I" forms!

| Dictionary form: | "I" form | "you" form | "you and I" form | "we" form |
|---|---|---|---|---|
| égnakA | _____ | _____ | _____ | _____ |
| _____ | _____ | _____ | _____ | éuŋglepi |
| _____ | éwauŋpe | _____ | _____ | _____ |
| otkéyA | _____ | _____ | _____ | _____ |

**12 a** Now you have to put everything away, but where does everything go? When your teacher tells you, put the object in the correct room, like the model. Say what you are doing while you are doing it.

Rooms: **olól'iȟ'aŋ, oásnikiye, oȟpáye, oíglužaža, owóte**

> **Pȟetížaŋžaŋ kiŋ oásnikiye kiŋ él égle yo.**

> **Ohaŋ, pȟetížaŋžaŋ kiŋ oásnikiye kiŋ él éwagle kte!**

**b** Now try this activity in a circle. Hold up your object. One of the other students will tell you where to put it. Take turns!

> **Lisa táku akhípȟa he? Héčhena Lakȟól wičhóthi kiŋ él úŋ he?**

**13** Skim through the dialogue below. What objects do Lisa and her mother talk about? Circle them!

Líla wamátukȟa! Iná nihíŋčiyewaye sél!
Haŋp'íkčeka kiŋ owáhiŋ kte. Héčhel
thiyáta waglí kte.

Iná: **Táku tókȟanuŋ he? Ináȟni! Owóhiŋsko yaškáŋ! Nitȟá-wožuha kiŋ tuktél yaŋká he?**

Lisa: **Slolwáye šni. Uŋgnáš haótkeye kiŋ mahél yaŋké.**

Iná: **Owáyawa wówapi kiŋ wáglutapi kiŋ akáŋl yaŋké. Éktuŋže šni ye!**

Lisa: **Mitȟá-ogle šóke kiŋ tuktél otká héči slolyáya he?**

Iná: **Haŋhépi otkéyaye šni! Oákaŋke háŋska kiŋ oȟláthe ȟpáye kečháŋmi. Thiíkčeya čík'ala waŋ yakáǧe k'uŋ nitȟá-oȟpáye él hé. Owáyawa kiŋ ektá ániŋ kte héčha he?**

Lisa: **Háŋ, éwaktuŋža tkȟá.**

Iná: **Nitȟá-ištamaza kiŋ wóžuha kiŋ mahél úŋ he?**

Lisa: **Háŋ, Iná! Iyúha waglúha kečháŋmi. Tókša ȟtayétu kiŋháŋ waŋčhíyaŋkiŋ kte!**

**14** Look back at the dialogue again. Where are Lisa's things? Can you finish the sentences below using the correct verbs?

Lisa tȟa-wóžuha kiŋ _____ kiŋ mahél _____.

Owáyawa wówapi kiŋ _____ kiŋ akáŋl _____.

Ógle šóke kiŋ _____ kiŋ oȟláthe _____.

Thiíkčeya čík'ala kiŋ _____ kiŋ él _____.

Lisa ištámaza kiŋ _____ kiŋ mahél _____.

Waŋná Lisa é na Bob táku tókȟuŋpi he?
Oyúblaye íyokhihe kiŋ ektá éslol'uŋyaŋpi kte.

**1** **a** Skim through the dialogue. What do Bob and Lisa talk about? Circle all of the correct pictures.

Bob: **Ho čha táku waŋláka he?**

Lisa: **Ho eyá, oyáte kiŋ éthipi. Thiíkčeya woslál églepi uŋspémakhiyapi.**

Bob: **Tuktél éthipi he?**

Lisa: **Obláye owáštečake čha hétu. Ikhíyela wakpála waŋ ȟpáye. Wakpála kiŋ aglágla čháŋ líla óta hé.**

Bob: **Ikhíyela ȟé waŋží yaŋká he?**

Lisa: **Hiyá, ȟé waŋžíni ikhíyela yaŋké šni. Ho éyaš wičhóthi kiŋ ilázata pahá waŋ yaŋké. Na pahá kiŋ iyóȟlathe blé čík'ala waŋ yaŋké.**

Bob: **Lečhála wičhóthi kiŋ lé míš-eyá waŋbláka wačhíŋ. Čha haŋp'íkčeka kiŋ hiyúmakhiya yo.**

Lisa: **Mitȟá-wóžuha kiŋ él úŋ. Čhaŋmáhel uŋyíŋ kte.**

Oháŋ, haŋp'íkčeka kiŋ hiyúmakhiya yo.

Má lé má! Waktá ečhúŋ we! Aŋpétu waŋží él akhé Tȟaté-Wiŋ waŋblákiŋ kta wačhíŋ. Okíyaka ye.

Tókša héčhamuŋ kte.

**1 b** What does the countryside look like near the village? **Read through the dialogue, and see if you can draw the scene as Lisa describes it.**

**2** Skim through the next part of the dialogue. What are the men of the village planning to do? **Circle the correct picture.**

Míla Kič'úŋ: **Tȟaŋháŋši! Yaglí čha líla iyómakiphi. Waŋnáš oyáte kiŋ uŋkígluwiŋyeyapi.**

Bob: **Táku tókȟa hwo?**

Míla Kič'úŋ: **Ečháŋni wanáse uŋyáŋpi kte. Níš-eyá óyapȟa oyákihi. Héčhel óuŋyakiyapi kte.**

Bob: **Haŋ, líla ówapȟa wačhiŋ! Ho éyaš wanásapi uŋmáspe šni.**

Míla Kič'úŋ: **Até wanása ohítike ló. Ho čha uŋspéničhiyiŋ kte. Ho po, kičhí wóuŋglakiŋ kte.**

Tȟašúŋke Ská: **Wanáš waŋyáŋg uŋyáhipi čha ičháŋtemawašte. Ečháŋni wanása uŋyáŋpi kte. Waŋúŋyaŋg nayážiŋpi kte. Tȟokátakiya níš-eyá uŋníspe kte.**

Bob: **Šuŋk'ákaŋyaŋkapi uŋmáspe, ho éyaš wanásapi waŋžíni él ówapȟa šni.**

Tȟašúŋke Ská: **Uŋkíye ób šuŋk'ákaŋnaŋkiŋ kte. Na tókhel ečhúŋk'uŋpi kiŋ iyéčhel ečhánuŋ kte.**

**3** If the sentence is true, circle **Háŋ**. If the sentence is not true, circle **Hiyá**.

Bob glí kiŋ hé uŋ Míla Kič'úŋ iyókišiče.  **Háŋ**  **Hiyá**

Bob taŋyáŋ wanásapi uŋspé.  **Háŋ**  **Hiyá**

Bob wanásapi uŋspé kta čhíŋ.  **Háŋ**  **Hiyá**

Bob šuŋk'ákaŋyaŋkapi uŋspé šni.  **Háŋ**  **Hiyá**

Míla Kič'úŋ atkúku kiŋ Bob uŋspékhiyiŋ kte.  **Háŋ**  **Hiyá**

## 4  Abléza po!

You already know how to say "you gave me something." Now let's look at how to say "you gave us something." Look at the dialogues below. James, Kimi, Summer and Matȟó will demonstrate.

**a** Which letters indicate "you --> me"? Underline them.

**b** Which letters indicate "you--> us"? Circle them.

Tȟaspáŋhaŋpi etáŋ mayák'u kta he?

Háŋ, tȟaspáŋhaŋpi etáŋ čhič'ú kte.

Asáŋpi etáŋ uŋyák'upi kta he?

Háŋ, asáŋpi etáŋ čhič'úpi kte.

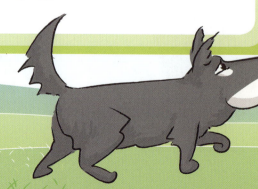

## 5 ⓐ Look at the mini-dialogues below, and draw lines from each one to the correct picture.

**1**
- Tȟabškátapi kiŋ ektá waŋmáyalaka he?
- Háŋ, waŋčhíyaŋke.

**2**
- Tȟabškátapi kiŋ ektá waŋúŋyalakapi he?
- Háŋ, waŋčhíyaŋkapi.

**3**
- Amáyaluptiŋ kta he?
- Hiyá, ačhíyuptiŋ kte šni!

**4**
- Uŋkáyaluptapi kta he?
- Hiyá, ačhíyuptapi kte šni!

**5**
- Mnikápȟopapi waŋží mayákahi he?
- Háŋ, mnikápȟopapi waŋ čhičáhi.

**6**
- Mnikápȟopapi etáŋ uŋyákahipi he?
- Mnikápȟopapi eyá čhičáhipi.

**7**
- Ómayakiyiŋ kta he?
- Háŋ, óčhičiyiŋ kte.

**8**
Óuŋyakiyapi kta he?
Háŋ, óčhičiyapi kte.

**9**
- Amáyaluta he?
- Hiyá, ačhíyuta šni!

**10**
- Uŋkáyalutapi he?
- Hiyá, ačhíyutapi šni!

**11**
- Mayáluȟičiŋ kta he?
- Háŋ, čhiyúȟičiŋ kte!

**12**
- Uŋyáluȟičapi kta he?
- Háŋ, čhiyúȟičapi kte!

**13**
- Wóuŋyak'upi kta he?
- Háŋ, wóčhič'upi kte.

**14**
- Wómayak'u kta he?
- Háŋ, wóčhič'u kte!

Remember that for you-->us, "y" stem verbs, like waŋYáŋkA, change to uŋ...yal, just like you-->me changes to mayal.

**ⓑ** Now, from the verb in the left hand column, draw a line to the correct dictionary form, and then to the picture that illustrates the meaning for each verb.

waŋúŋyalakapi     ayúta

uŋkáyaluptapi     ókiyA

uŋyákahipi     kahí

uŋkáyalutapi     ayúptA

uŋyáluȟičapi     waŋyáŋkA

óuŋyakiyapi     yuȟíčA

**6** Get in a circle with your classmates. Your teacher will give each of you one or two pictures of things to eat or drink (photocopied from page 149). Practice asking and answering what "you brought us" like the model.

Táku uŋyákahipi he?           Tȟaspáŋ eyá čhičáhipi.

**7** Stay in the circle with your classmates. Let's talk about "What time will you wake us up?" One of you will speak for the group. This person will call on someone to answer. Look at the models, and decide when you need to wake up! You can use all the days of the week, and tomorrow, as you talk.

> Híŋhaŋni kiŋháŋ owáyawa-ta uŋyáŋpi kte héčha. Owápȟe šakówiŋ kiŋháŋ uŋyáluȟičapi kta he?

> Háŋ, owápȟe šakówiŋ kiŋháŋ čhiyúȟičapi kte!

> Owáŋkayužažapi kiŋ owáyawa-ta uŋyáŋpi kte šni! Owápȟe akéwaŋži kiŋ uŋyáluȟičapi kta he?

> Háŋ, owápȟe akéwaŋži kiŋháŋ čhiyúȟičapi kte!

7:00    11:00

**8 a** Where did you see us? Get into groups of three. Imagine that you have all been walking around town. Take turns: Two of you will ask the third, like the models.

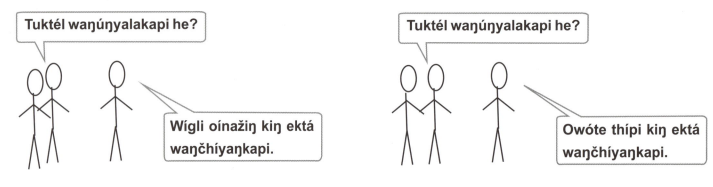

> Tuktél waŋúŋyalakapi he?

> Wígli oínažiŋ kiŋ ektá waŋčhíyaŋkapi.

> Tuktél waŋúŋyalakapi he?

> Owóte thípi kiŋ ektá waŋčhíyaŋkapi.

**b** Now, write sentences on scratch paper about "who saw us," like the models. Write three sentences on a piece of scrap paper, like the models below.

Susan wígli oínažiŋ kiŋ ektá waŋúŋyaŋkapi.
Peter owóte thípi kiŋ ektá waŋúŋyaŋkapi.

**9 a** Look back at the dialogue on page 85 (activity 2). Find all the verbs that talk about "you --> us" Write them here:

1. _____

2. _____

**b** What does this verb "**uŋspéničhiyiŋ**" talk about? Circle the correct answer.

we--->you          he--->you

me--->you

**10** Skim through the dialogue below where Tȟašúŋke Ská talks about the activities done in preparation for the buffalo hunt. Then number the images in the order in which Tȟašúŋke Ská mentions the activities.

Bob: **Lakȟóta oyáte kiŋ tókhel wanásapi he?**

Tȟašúŋke Ská: **Tȟoká tuŋwéya kiŋ ptéȟčaka kiŋ owíčhale yápi kte.**

**Toháŋl ptéȟčaka etáŋ waŋwíčhayaŋkapi kiŋháŋ kúpi kte. Toháŋl glípi kiŋháŋ uŋkígluwiŋyeyapi kte. Tȟoká šúŋkawakȟáŋ kiŋ wíwičhuŋyuŋpi kte.**

Bob: **Ho na heháŋl táku tókȟuŋk'uŋpi kta he?**

Tȟašúŋke Ská: **Toháŋl šúŋkawakȟáŋ kiŋ wíwičhayuŋ uŋkígluštaŋpi kiŋháŋ uŋkíš-eyá ité kiŋ wíuŋkiyuŋpi kte.**

**Toháŋl ité kiŋ wíkiyuŋ uŋkígluštaŋpi kiŋháŋ itázipa na waŋhíŋkpe kiŋ uŋkíkikčupi kte.**

**Toháŋl wípȟe kiŋ uŋkíkikčupi kiŋháŋ wičháša wakȟáŋ kiŋ azíl'uŋyaŋpi kte.**

**Toháŋl azíl'uŋyaŋpi kiŋ iglúštaŋ kiŋháŋ wanása uŋkíyayapi kte.**

Bob: **Čha míš táku tókȟamuŋ kta hwo?**

Tȟašúŋke Ská: **Óuŋyakiyapi kte. Niyé kȟó uŋyáŋpi kte. Uŋkíhakab níŋ kte. Tȟóéyaš waŋúŋyaŋg nayážiŋpi kte.**

## 11  Abléza po!

**a**  Look at the two sentences below.

    **Yaglí kte.** (You will come back.)

    **Waúŋyutiŋ kte.** (You and I will eat.)

**b**  What happens when we connect the sentences? Look at the single sentence below, and compare it to the two separate sentences above. What words do we add when we connect the two sentences? Circle them.

    **Toháŋl yaglí kiŋháŋ, waúŋyutiŋ kte.** (When you come back, you and I will eat.)

**č**  When are they doing the two activities?  Circle the correct answer.

    **Now.**        **In the past.**        **In the future.**

**12**  Now go back to the dialogue. Read through it again, and finish the sentences with the correct next step, according to what Tȟašúŋke-ska said.

**Toháŋl tuŋwéya kiŋ glípi kiŋháŋ iglúwiŋyeyapi kte.**

**a**  Toháŋl šúŋkawakȟáŋ kiŋ wíwičhayuŋpi kiŋháŋ _____.

**b**  Toháŋl itázipa kiŋ ikíkčupi kiŋháŋ _____.

**č**  Toháŋl wičháša wakȟáŋ kiŋ azílwičhaye kiŋháŋ _____.

**13**  Today's children have chores to do also, then it's time for fun! Let's help them write some sentences about what they will do. Look at the model, and then write 5 more sentences about what the children will do when the chores are done! You can draw pictures, too!

MODEL: **Toháŋl šúŋka čheslí pahí iglúštaŋpi kiŋháŋ, wičhítenaškaŋškaŋ waŋyáŋg yaŋkápi kte.**

**14** **a** How about you? You will probably have to do homework after school, but then what? Look at the suggestions for activities, and then ask 3 people what they will do, like the model. Take notes!

> Toháŋl thiyáta wówaši ečhánuŋ kiŋháŋ, heháŋl táku tókȟanuŋ kta he?

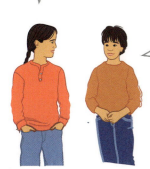

> Toháŋl thiyáta wówaši ečhámuŋ kiŋháŋ, heháŋl wanúŋwiŋ kte.

> Here are some ideas!
>
> | | |
> |---|---|
> | wičhítenaškaŋškaŋ | wawákšu kte. |
> | waŋyáŋg maŋkíŋ kte. | tȟabwáškatiŋ kte. |
> | šuŋk'ákaŋmaŋkiŋ kte. | wówapi blawá kte. |
> | howákhuwa kte. | waškátiŋ kte. |

**b** What did your classmates tell you? Look back at your notes, and write 3 sentences about what they will do when they have finished studying.

Model: Susan toháŋl thiyáta tȟawówaši kiŋ iglúštaŋ kiŋháŋ, heháŋl škátiŋ kte.

**15** **a** When you are grown up, what will you do? Look at the model dialogue, and the suggestions for jobs you might have. Then ask 3 people. Take notes!

Person 1: **(Toháŋl) Iníčhaǧe kiŋháŋ, táku heníčha kta he?**
Person 2: **(Toháŋl) Imáčhaǧe kiŋháŋ, iyéčhiŋkyaŋka aphíye hemáčha kte.**

| | |
|---|---|
| akíčhita | oyáŋke itȟáŋčhaŋ |
| wówapikaǧe | wóhela |
| waúŋspewičhakhiye | hayápi wíyopȟeye |
| pteyúha wičháša/wíŋyaŋ | onákasni wičháša/wíŋyaŋ |
| čhaŋksáyuha/wawóyuspa | iwátȟokšu tȟáŋka kaȟápe |
| pȟoǧó wičháša/wíŋyaŋ | |

> By the way, in everyday speech, **toháŋl** can be skipped. Look at the model sentence here, and compare it with the pattern you have been practicing.

**b** Now, write a short paragraph about what you want to do when you grow up, and about what your classmates want to do. Your paragraph should have at least 4 sentences.

Toháŋl wičháša kiŋ Lakȟóta wičhóthi kiŋ él iglúwiŋyeyapi kiŋháŋ, táku tókȟuŋpi kta he? Iyéuŋyaŋpi kte!

**16** The scouts have found some buffalo! Skim through the dialogue. How many of the buffalo are lying down? Write the number here: _____

Tuŋwéya: **Ptéȟčaka kiŋ iyéwičhuŋyaŋpi. Líla ótapi na kaíyuzeyakel ománipi.**

Tȟašúŋke Ská: **Táku tókȟuŋpi hwo?**

Tuŋwéya: **Ptéȟčaka kiŋ iyúha kiníl wayášla-haŋpi. Húŋȟ wayátȟe-kuŋs ȟpáyapi. Húŋȟ ičáptaŋptaŋ kič'úŋpi. Bloká kiŋ čónala kičhízapi. Ptéȟčaka kiŋ óta čhebčhépapi. Ptehíŋčala kiŋ tónakel naháŋȟčiŋ azíŋpi, čha húŋkupi kiŋ wičhákhutepi šni yo. Ptéȟčaka kiŋ waŋžíni hušté šni.**

Tȟašúŋke Ská: **Wanása uŋkíyayapi kte héčha. Waŋná. Bob, lé šúŋkawakȟáŋ kiŋ akáŋyaŋka yo. Mihákab ú wo.**

**17** Now read through the dialogue again, and decide whether the statements below are true (**Háŋ!**) or false (**Hiyá!**).

Ptéȟčaka kiŋ waŋžíni wayášlapi šni.        Háŋ! / Hiyá!

Húŋȟ ikpáptaŋptaŋ.        Háŋ! / Hiyá!

Bloká kiŋ óta kičhízapi.        Háŋ! / Hiyá!

Ptéȟčaka kiŋ čónala čhebčhépapi.        Háŋ! / Hiyá!

Ptehíŋčala kiŋ tónakel azíŋpi.        Háŋ! / Hiyá!

Ptéȟčaka kiŋ iyúha kiníl hušté.        Háŋ! / Hiyá!

Hókahé! Wanáuŋsapi kte!

# Buffalo Hunt - Wóuŋspe 11

**1** A very successful hunt is finished! Bob is helping the Lakota men count the kill. Skim through what Bob and Míla Kič'úŋ are saying, and write the number of buffalo each man killed next to his picture.

 —  —  —  —  —

 —  —  —  —  —

Bob: **Ičhéwiŋškaš ptéȟčaka óta wičháopi ka!**

Míla Kič'úŋ: **Háŋ. Taŋyáŋ wawáŋyaŋg nayážiŋ he? Tuwá héčhuŋpi héči waŋwíčhalaka he?**

Bob: **Háŋ, wičháša waŋ líla čhépe kiŋ ptéȟčaka yámni wičháo.**

Míla Kič'úŋ: **Itéšniyaŋ?**

Bob: **Wičháša waŋ líla oówaŋyaŋg wašté kiŋ ptéȟčaka núŋm wičháo. Wičháša waŋ ité kiŋ él osnáze kiŋ ptéȟčaka tób wičháo. Wičháša waŋ šuŋksápa waŋ akáŋyaŋke kiŋ ptéȟčaka waŋžíla ó.**

Míla Kič'úŋ: **Wáŋ!**

Bob: **Wičháša waŋ wíyaka núŋm pȟégnake kiŋ ptéȟčaka waŋžíni ó šni. Wičháša waŋ iphíyaka kšúpi waŋ úŋ kiŋ ptéȟčaka núŋm wičháo. Wičháša waŋ Tȟašúŋke Ská čhiŋkšíye kiŋ ptéȟčaka záptaŋ wičháo.**

Míla Kič'úŋ: **Wičáyakȟe séče.**

Bob: **Wičháša waŋ ité tȟokíye kiŋ ptéȟčaka núŋm wičháo. Wičháša waŋ ité šakíye kiŋ ptéȟčaka waŋžíni ó šni. Wičháša waŋ líla ptéčela kiŋ ptéȟčaka yámni wičháo.**

Míla Kič'úŋ: **Níš-eyá waŋží yaó kéčhaŋmi. Ho po, éwaŋuŋyaŋkiŋ kte.**

**2** Read through the dialogue on pg 93 again. How many buffalo were killed overall?

a. 22      b. 23      č. 25

## 3   Abléza po!

Look at these two sentences.

**Wičháša waŋ ptéȟčaka núŋm wičhákte.**

**Wičháša kiŋ líla háŋske.**

Now look at how we put them together:

**Wičháša waŋ líla háŋske kiŋ ptéȟčaka núŋm wičhákte.**

[[Head] [description of the head]] [main part of the sentence]

The man    who is very tall    killed two buffalo.

First circle the parts. Then write their names on the line below each sentence.

**Wičhíŋčala waŋ líla ptéčela kiŋ hí.**

_____

**Thípi waŋ tȟó kiŋ mitȟáwa.**

_____

**4** Can you write single sentences with the parts below? Write your sentences below. Remember that ablaut verbs need to change to "**e**" before **kiŋ**!

Model: **Čháŋčheǧa waŋ awáhi. Líla tȟáŋka.**    *Čháŋčheǧa waŋ líla tȟáŋka kiŋ awáhi.*

1. **Šúŋkawakȟáŋ waŋ mak'ú. Líla lúzahe.** _____

2. **Wówapi waŋ blawá. Líla háŋske.** _____

3. **Omás'apȟela waŋ opȟétȟuŋ. Líla othéȟike.** _____

4. **Wíŋyaŋ waŋ čépȟaŋšiwaye. Misákhib nážiŋ.** _____

5. **Tȟaspáŋ waŋ wáte. Oyúl šíče.** _____

6. **Waúŋspewičhakhiya waŋ waštéčake. Kál thí.** _____

7. **Šúŋka waŋ líla očhíŋšiče. Kál thí.** _____

8. **Hokšíla waŋ wayázaŋ othí-ta áyapi. Hiŋȟpáye.** _____

## 5  Abléza po!

**a** Look at the two sentences, and then the combined, single sentence. This sentence is plural. Notice that the verb in the descriptive part must be pluralized. This means that it will have reduplication or "pi" or both (when referring to body parts or bodies).

Hokšíla eyá glípi.
Hokšíla kiŋ háŋskaskapi.

Hokšíla eyá háŋskaskapi kiŋ glípi.
[[Head] [description of the head]] [main part].
[[The boys][who are very tall]][have come back].

**b** Now look at the sentences below. Can you once again circle the parts, and label them under each sentence?

Wičíŋčala eyá líla oȟ'áŋwaštepi kiŋ iyáyapi.

_____

Oákaŋke eyá šašá kiŋ awáhi.

_____

Ptewániyaŋpi eyá gleškáškapi kiŋ waŋwíčhayaŋkapi.

_____

**6** **a** Write single sentences with the parts below, like the model. Write your sentences on the lines provided in the book so that you can use them for part b.

Model: **Wíyatke eyá ahípi. Tȟaŋkíŋkiŋyaŋ. ==>** Wíyatke eyá tȟaŋkíŋkiŋyaŋ kiŋ ahípi.

1. **Pšitȟó eyá mak'ú wo. Tȟotȟó.**  _____

2. **Ičábu eyá ahí. Líla háŋskaska.**  _____

3. **Šúŋkawakȟáŋ eyá awíčhahipi. Skaskápi.** _____

4. **Wičhása eyá hél mníčiyapi. Líla ksápapi.** _____

5. **Wapȟóštaŋla eyá opȟéwatȟuŋ. Tȟotȟó.** _____

6. **Tȟaspáŋ eyá opȟétȟuŋ. Šašá.**  _____

7. **Wóžuha eyá k'íŋ. Líla tketké.**  _____

8. **Šuŋȟpála eyá iwíčhaču. Líla čhepčhépapi.** _____

**b** Now look at the sentences you wrote. Is the head animate or inanimate? Mark each sentence with an "A" or an "I." Then, circle the pluralization in each sentence ("**pi**" or reduplication or both).

## 7 Abléza po!

**a** Look at the sentences below, and then at the single, combined sentence. Notice that the descriptive part is in this case a long sentence.

Wičháša waŋ ptéȟčaka waŋžíla kté.
Wičháša kiŋ šuŋksápa waŋ akáŋyaŋke.

Wičháša waŋ šuŋksápa waŋ akáŋyaŋke kiŋ ptéȟčaka waŋžíla kté.
[[head] [description of the head]] [main part].
[[The man] [who was riding a black horse]] [killed only one buffalo].

**b** Now look at the two sentences below. Can you circle the parts and label them below each sentence?

Hokšíla eyá wačhípi kiŋ él ópȟapi kiŋ waŋná ípuzapi.

_____

Wíŋyaŋ eyá wičháȟpi owíŋža kiŋ lé káǧapi kiŋ hená uŋčíwičhawaye.

_____

**8a** The children are drawing animals that they have around their hometown. First, draw lines to match the animals on the left with the descriptions on the right.

kiŋyé šni úŋ
taŋyáŋ kiŋyé
asáŋpi yuslípi
siŋté blaská
thukíha sutá
nakpá háŋskaska
pȟahíŋ pȟepȟé
wašúŋ othí
hú šaglóǧaŋ
kignúŋg hokhúwa
Lakȟóta kiŋ wičhákhuwapi
Lakȟóta kiŋ akáŋyaŋkapi
Lakȟóta kiŋ wíyaka kiŋ pȟégnakapi

**8 b** Now, write a sentence about each animal on a piece of scrap paper, like the model:
Ziŋtkála waŋ kiŋyé šni úŋ kiŋ hé waglékšuŋ héčha.

**č** Then work with a partner. Make a question with the description and ask your partner about the animals, like the model below.

> Ziŋtkála waŋ kiŋyé šni úŋ kiŋ hé táku he?

> Ziŋtkála waŋ kiŋyé šni úŋ kiŋ hé waglékšuŋ héčha.

**9 a** Look at the pictures below. Select two of them, and write sentences, like the model:
Hokšíla waŋ ógle zí waŋ úŋ kiŋ wiŋčhíŋčala waŋ isákhib yaŋké.

① ② ③ ④ ⑤

**b** Then, read your sentences to a partner. Can she or he guess which picture you were writing about?

> Hokšíla waŋ uŋzóǧe tȟózi waŋ úŋ kiŋ wíŋyaŋ waŋ isákhib yaŋké.

> Lé tȟokáheya kiŋ hé é! Lé ičínuŋpa kiŋ hé é!

**č** Now, try this in your class! One person will say a sentence about someone in the room. The rest of you guess who s/he is talking about!

> Wičhíŋčala waŋ háŋpa skaská waŋ úŋ kiŋ Patti ihákab yaŋké.

> Hé Susan é!

**10** **a** Look at the picture on pages 22 and 23. Write 3 questions about the people or animals in the picture, like the model:

Hokšíla waŋ šuŋk'ákaŋyaŋke kiŋ hé tuktél úŋ he?

**b** Next, ask a partner. Your partner will answer you by pointing at the correct figure.

> Hokšíla waŋ šuŋk'ákaŋyaŋke kiŋ hé tuktél úŋ he?

> Hokšíla kiŋ hé lél úŋ.

# 11  Abléza po!

**a** Look at this dialogue below.
Who knows the horse?

Al: **Šúŋkawakȟáŋ waŋ líla lúzahaŋ čha opȟéwatȟuŋ.**
(I bought **a** horse that is really fast.)
Joe: **Itéšniyaŋ, waŋbláka wačhíŋ.**

Circle the correct answer.
1) only Al
2) only Joe
3) both Al and Joe
4) neither of the two

**b** Look at the new dialogue below.
Who knows the horse now?

Al: **Šúŋkawakȟáŋ waŋ opȟéwatȟuŋ kiŋ hé lé é.**
(This is **the** horse that I bought.)
Joe: **Oówaŋyaŋg wašté!**

Circle the correct answer.
1) only Al
2) only Joe
3) both Al and Joe
4) neither of the two

**12** Look at the dialogues below.  Who knows the thing or person being talked about? Circle the correct answer for each dialogue.

**a** Pete: **Čháŋčheǧa waŋ líla hó wašté čha wakáǧe.**
David:  **Khilí. Waŋbláka wačhíŋ. Mayákipazo kta he?**

       1) only Peter     2) only David     3) both     4) neither of the two

**b** Mary: **Šúŋka waŋ hokšíla waŋ yaȟtáke kiŋ hé oyúspapi.**
Janet:  **Oháŋ, wašté.**

       1) only Mary     2) only Janet     3) both     4) neither of the two

**č** Cynthia: **Ziŋtkála waŋ líla šá čha waŋbláke.**
Jim:  **Itéšniyaŋ.**

       1) only Cynthia     2) only Jim     3) both     4) neither of the two

**e** Allen: **Hokšíla eyá yuphíya lowáŋpi kiŋ hená hípi.**
Avery:  **Nakéš. Awíčhapȟe uŋyáŋkape ló.**

       1) only Allen     2) only Avery     3) both     4) neither of the two

# 13 Abléza po!

In the sentences below note that when the description is followed by **čha** then the English sentence has "a". When it is followed with **kiŋ** then the English sentence has "the".

**Šúŋkawakȟáŋ waŋ líla lúzahaŋ čha opȟéwatȟuŋ.**
(I bought **a** horse that is very fast.)

**Šúŋkawakȟáŋ waŋ líla lúzahe kiŋ opȟéwatȟuŋ.**
(I bought **the** horse that is very fast.)

To show that "**čha**" or "**kiŋ**" refer to the head, connect them using arrows, like the model above.

**Wapȟóštaŋ waŋ sápa čha opȟéwatȟuŋ.**
(I bought a hat that is black.)

**Wapȟóštaŋ waŋ sápe kiŋ opȟéwatȟuŋ.**
(I bought the hat that is black.)

Very important in Lakota! The head (horse/hat) is *always* followed by an indefinite article (such as **waŋ, waŋží, eyá, etáŋ**).

**14** Read the sentences below. Based on the translation, decide whether each sentence should have "**kiŋ**" or "**čha**," and finish the sentence.

a. Wapȟóštaŋ waŋ sápa _____ opȟéwatȟuŋ.                = I bought a hat that is black.

b. Omás'apȟela waŋží ská _____ wačhíŋ.                 = I want a cell phone that is white.

č. Wičháȟpi owíŋža waŋ líla wašté _____ káǧe.          = She made a star quilt that is very pretty.

e. Hokšíla waŋ líla yuphíya wačhí _____ hé Jim ečíyapi. = The boy who dances so well is called Jim.

g. Wówapi eyá yawá-phiča _____ ahípi.                  = They brought some books that are good to read.

ǧ. Šúŋka waŋ wayáȟtake šni _____ yuhá-phiča.           = It is good to have a dog that doesn't bite.

h. Wazí eyá líla háŋskaska _____ iyóȟlathe yaŋkápi.    = They sat under some pine trees that were very tall.

ȟ. Wakpá waŋ líla šmá _____ él ípi.                    = They arrived at a river that was very deep.

i. Wičhíŋčala eyá Waŋblí Pahá ektá thí _____ hená ób wóglake. = She spoke to the girls who live in Eagle Butte.

k. Olówaŋ etáŋ onáȟ'uŋ waštéšte _____ owále kte.       = I am going to look for some songs that sound good.

**15** The men with the hunting party are part of Míla Kič'úŋ's extended family. Look at the sentences describing the kinship between Míla's father and the men from the hunt. Then, rewrite the sentences to show how the men are related to Míla himself, like the model:

**ⓐ** Wičháša waŋ ité kiŋ él osnáze kiŋ Tȟašúŋke Ská atéye.

_Wičháša waŋ líla ité kiŋ él osnáze kiŋ Míla Kič'úŋ tȟuŋkášitku._

**ⓑ** Wičháša waŋ líla oówaŋyaŋg wašté kiŋ Tȟašúŋke Ská čhiyéye.

_____

**ⓒ** Wičháša waŋ líla čhépe kiŋ Tȟašúŋke Ská suŋkáye.

_____

**ⓔ** Wičháša waŋ šuŋksápa waŋ akáŋyaŋke kiŋ Tȟašúŋke Ská tȟuŋškáye.

_____

**ⓖ** Wičháša waŋ iphíyaka kšúpi waŋ úŋ kiŋ Tȟašúŋke Ská čhiŋkšítku.

_____

**ⓖ** Wičháša waŋ wíyaka núŋm pȟégnake kiŋ Tȟašúŋke Ská suŋkáye.

_____

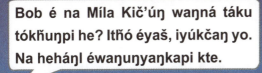

Bob é na Míla Kič'úŋ waŋná táku tókȟuŋpi he? Itȟó éyaš, iyúkčaŋ yo. Na heháŋl éwaŋuŋyaŋkapi kte.

**16** Now it is evening, and the men are sitting at the fire talking about the hunt! Skim through the dialogue below. Which of the boys -- Míla Kič'úŋ or Bob -- killed his first buffalo on this hunt?

Write your answer here: _____

Tȟašúŋke Ská: **Líla taŋyáŋ wanáuŋsapi. Ptéȟčaka waŋ yaó kiŋ hé čík'ala éyaš taŋyéla čhépe, tȟuŋšká. Taŋyáŋ ečhánuŋ weló.**

Míla Kič'úŋ: **Ósmaka waŋ ópta íŋyaŋkapi k'uŋ héhaŋ líla wókȟokipȟe. Ičhíŋ iǧúǧa eyá tȟaŋkíŋkiŋyaŋ kiŋ šúŋkawakȟáŋ kiŋ aȟíčahaŋpi. Išníkal éš tuwéni hiŋȟpáye šni.**

Bob: **Háŋ, líla wókȟokipȟe, éyaš aígluštaŋ šuŋk'ákaŋuŋyaŋkapi. Wičháša waŋ ité kiŋ él osnáze kiŋ hé táku ečíyapi he?**

Míla Kič'úŋ: **Čhetáŋ Khuwá ečíyapi.**

Bob: **Ptéȟčaka waŋ tȟokáheya íŋyaŋke kiŋ hé ó. Ptéȟčaka k'uŋ hé hiŋȟpáye k'uŋ héhaŋ uŋmá kiŋ oíč'uŋnil hiŋglápi. Na heháŋl okȟúl-waštépi.**

Tȟašúŋke Ská: **Tȟuŋšká, níš líla taŋyáŋ ečhánuŋ weló. Kȟoškálaka waŋží tȟokáheya ptéȟčaka waŋží ó čháŋna oyáte kiŋ uŋyúonihaŋpi s'a. Ho čha toháŋl wapȟál uŋkígluštaŋpi kiŋháŋ Ȟé Sápa-ta uŋkániyaŋpi kte. Uŋkípi kiŋháŋ wičhóȟ'aŋ wakȟáŋ waŋ uŋkáǧapi kte. Čhažé waŋží uŋníč'upi kte.**

Bob: **Wóphila ečhíčiye ló.**

**17** Read through the dialogue on page 101 again, and answer the questions.

**a** Ptéȟčaka waŋ Bob tȟokáheya ó kiŋ hé tókheča he?

1) Tȟamáheča na húŋkešni.
2) Čík'ala na tȟamáheča.
3) Čík'ala na čhépe.

**b** Ósmaka kiŋ él táku tókȟuŋpi he?

1) Ptéȟčaka óta wičháopi.
2) Tuwéni hiŋȟpáye šni.
3) Bob čhažé waŋ k'úpi.

**č** Wičháša waŋ Čhetáŋ Khuwá kiŋ hé tuwé he?

1) Wičháša waŋ wíyaka núŋm pȟégnake kiŋ hé é.
2) Wičháša waŋ šuŋgsápa waŋ akáŋyaŋke k'uŋ hé é.
3) Wičháša waŋ ité kiŋ él osnáze kiŋ hé é.

**e** Ptéȟčaka waŋ tȟokáheya íŋyaŋke kiŋ hé tuwá ó he?

1) Tȟašúŋke Ská.
2) Míla Kič'úŋ.
3) Čhetáŋ Khuwá.

**g** Ptéȟčaka waŋ tȟokáheya ópi kiŋ hiŋȟpáye k'uŋ héhaŋ uŋmá kiŋ táku tókȟuŋpi he?

1) Uŋmá kiŋ napȟápi.
2) Uŋmá kiŋ watúkȟa áyapi.
3) Uŋmá kiŋ khúl iyúŋkapi.

**ǧ** Bob yuónihaŋpi kta čha tókhiya yápi kta he?

1) Matȟó Thípila-ta.
2) Ȟé Sápa-ta.
3) Íŋyaŋša Oók'e-ta.

**h** Ȟé Sápa-ta iyáyapi šni haŋni táku tókȟuŋpi kta he?

1) Ptéȟčaka kiŋ wičháopi kte.
2) Waŋhíŋkpe kiŋ gluwíŋyeyapi kte.
3) Wapȟátapi kte.

**ȟ** Ȟesápa kiŋ ektá táku tókȟuŋpi kta he?

1) Wičhóȟ'aŋ wakȟáŋ waŋží kágapi na Bob Lakȟól'iya čhaštȟúŋpi kte.
2) Wičhóȟ'aŋ wakȟáŋ waŋží kágapi na ptéȟčaka etáŋ wičhákhutepi kte.
3) Wičhóȟ'aŋ wakȟáŋ waŋží kágapi na pȟežíȟota etáŋ pahípi kte.

Lakȟóta oyáte kiŋ Bob Ȟesápa-ta áyapi. Hél táku akhípȟa kte kiŋ slolyáya yačhíŋ he? Éslol'uŋyaŋpi kte ló.

**1** Míla Kič'úŋ's family is getting ready to leave for the Black Hills. Read through the dialogue and circle the items that Míla's mother asks them to bring over to pack on the travois.

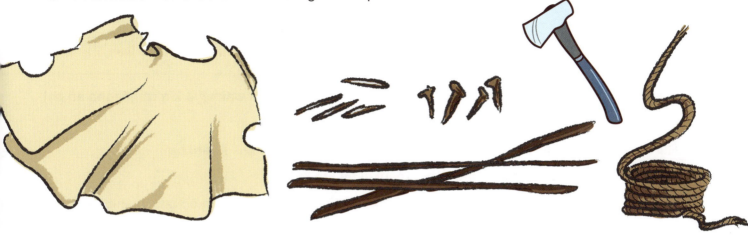

Húŋku: **Hupáwaheyuŋpi kiŋ bluwíŋyeya. Čhiŋkší, tȟošká, táku kiŋ iyúha aú ómakiya pe. Tȟokáheya wakhéya kiŋ aú pe.**

Míla Kič'úŋ: **Oháŋ, iná, uŋkáupi kte.**

Húŋku: **Čhuŋkší, wičhéškipasise kiŋ aú we.**

Tȟaté Wiŋ: **Oháŋ, iná, awáu kte.**

Bob: **Míš thušú kiŋ hená awáu kte.**

Húŋku: **Hiyá, hená aú šni ye, líla tketké. Éeye wihúŋpaspa kiŋ aú we.**

**2** Now it's your turn! Pretend that you and your classmates are going on a trip!

a. First, your teacher will ask you to bring all the things you will need from a pile of pictures or objects.

b. Next, take turns asking your classmates to bring the things you will need!

**Paílepi kiŋ aú we!**

**Thiyóbleča kiŋ aú wo!**

**3** Míla's mother has returned to check the travois! Let's see what happened! Read through the dialogue, and fill in the chart that follows.

Húŋku: **Čhiŋkší, čhéǧa kiŋ ayáhi he?**

MK: **Háŋ, iná, čhéǧa kiŋ awáhi yeló.**

Húŋku: **Wakhéya kiŋ íŋš tók? Bob kičhí ayáhi he?**

MK: **Hiyá, iná, naháŋȟčiŋ. Maštíŋčala waŋ íŋyaŋg hiyáya čha waŋúŋyaŋkapi. Bob íčat'a ločhíŋ čha uŋkhútepe ló. Na nakúŋ uŋkópe ló.**

Húŋku: **Niȟ'áŋhipe! Ečháŋni uŋkíyayapi kte héčha kštó. Ho čha wakhéya kiŋ wáŋčagna aú pe!**

MK: **Oháŋ, uŋkáupi kte.**

Húŋku: **Wičhéškipasise kiŋ hená íŋš tók? Hená kȟó waŋbláke šni. Ayáhi he?**

MK: **Hiyá, iná, hená awáhi šni. Ičhíŋ tȟaŋkší aú kta kéye.**

Húŋku: **Má k'éya! Wakȟáŋȟeža, táku kiŋ iyúha wáŋčag aú pe! Táku kiŋ čónala ayáhipi k'éyaš ečháŋni uŋkíyayapi kte.**

Items the children have brought already:

_____

_____

Items the children still need to bring:

_____

_____

**4  Abléza po!**

Look at the list of verbs below. What is added to the verbs of "coming" to make the verbs of "bringing"? Write your answer here: _____

ú  -----> aú

hí  ------> ahí

Read the sentences below and answer the two questions that follow.

**Híŋhaŋni thušú eyá awáhi.**       **Ȟtálehaŋ šúŋkawakȟáŋ waŋ awáhi.**
**Čháŋčheǧa waŋží aú wo.**        **Oháŋ, čháŋčheǧa waŋží awáu kte.**

Which of the two verbs do we use in commands or in future activities? Write it here: _____

Which of the two verbs do we use when the activity is already finished? Write it here: _____

**5** Your teacher will put a number of pictures or items on one side of the room. Work with a partner. One of you will ask the other to bring something. The one who is doing the action will say what s/he will do before doing it. Then, s/he will say what s/he has done after doing it, like the models.

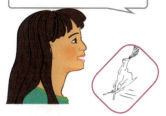

Tȟáȟča kiŋ aú we.

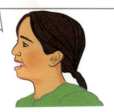

Oháŋ, tȟáȟča kiŋ awáu kte.

Tȟáȟča kiŋ awáhi.

**6** Now the village has reached the Black Hills, and set up camp. Here, to honor Bob's first kill, they will give him a name, and some special gifts. Everyone who will give Bob a gift is taking the items to the center of the village. Skim through the dialogue below and circle the items that are mentioned.

Tȟašúŋke Ská: **Bob itázipa mitȟáwa kiŋ waŋží uŋ tȟatȟáŋka kiŋ ó. Ho čha wak'ú kta wačhíŋ. Čhiŋkší, hóčhoka-ta áya yo.**

Čhetáŋ Khuwá: **Wašté! Míš waŋhíŋkpe etáŋ otúwakiȟ'aŋ kte. Čhiŋkší, waŋhíŋkpe kiŋ lená hóčhoka-ta áya yo.**

Čhetáŋ Khuwá na kȟoláku: **Lakȟóta kȟoškálaka iyóhila očhósya ištíŋmapi kta iyéčhetu. Ho čha ptehíŋšma kiŋ lé uŋk'úpi kte. Hóčhoka-ta uŋkáyapi kte ló.**

Tȟaté Wiŋ Húŋku: **Míš nakúŋ Lisa takúŋl wak'ú kta wačhíŋ. Bob kaáyiŋ kte. Tȟaté-Wiŋ, čhaŋkȟóžuha waŋ tȟoyéla ȟčiŋ kšúpi kiŋ hé hóčhoka-ta áya ye.**

Tȟašúŋke Ská: **Ho waŋná Lakȟól'iya čhaš'úŋtȟuŋpi šni haŋní iníuŋkağapi kte héčha yeló.**

**7** Read through the dialogue again. For each of the gifts mentioned, draw a line from the item to the person or persons who will give it. Be careful! Not all of the items pictured below were mentioned in the dialogue!

**8** **Abléza po!**

To the right is a list of verbs of bringing and taking.

1) Match them with the verbs of coming and going.
2) One of the bringing/taking verbs is slightly different, circle it. Can you tell what is different about it?

| | |
|---|---|
| aú | í |
| ahí | ú |
| aí | yÁ |
| áyA | glí |
| aglí | hí |

**9** Let's pretend that you are going to have a give-away in your classroom. Each of you will contribute one or two items. You can use things you have, or your teacher will give you pictures of things to give. Take turns asking and taking the things to the center of your classroom, like the models.

Wóžuha kiŋ lé hóčhoka-ta áya yo!

Oháŋ, ámniŋ kte!

**10** Many of the hunters, and some other villagers, are giving gifts, and they are taking them to the center of the village. Work in pairs. Partner one should look at page 151 and partner two on page 152. Ask your partner questions to figure out the missing gifts! Complete your picture by drawing in the missing items next to the people taking them. Use the models to help you.

**11** Now look at the map you have finished, and write sentences about who is taking which items to the center of the village, like the model. Remember, some items are being taken by more than one person.

Tȟaté Wíŋ haŋp'íkčeka kšúpi kiŋ hóčhoka-ta áye.

_____

_____

_____

_____

_____

## 12 Abléza po!

You know the root verbs **yÁ** (to be going there) and **í** (to have gone there, arrived at a place away from here). Now look at these two verbs with the "a-" prefix: **áyA** and **aí**. Read the sentences below, and answer the questions.

> Ȟtálehaŋ até iyéčhiŋkyaŋke kiŋ wígli oínažiŋ-ta aí.
>
> Haŋhépi owíŋ eyá wačhípi-ta wíyopȟewayiŋ kta čha awái.
>
> Waŋná wačhípi-ta wóyute kiŋ lé áble.
>
> Híŋhaŋni kiŋháŋ thiyóblečha kiŋ lé uŋčí thí kiŋ ektá ámniŋ kte.
>
> Ičábu kiŋ lená wačhípi-ta áya yo.
>
> Nikȟúŋši wačhípi-ta áya yo.
>
> Ȟtálehaŋ mitȟákoža kiŋ otȟúŋwahe-ta awíčhawai.

Which of the verbs describes a future action, something ongoing, or a command?

Circle the correct answer:     **áyA     aí**

Which of the verbs says that the taking is already finished?          **áyA     aí**

**13** Many people were taking gifts to the center of the village for Bob and Lisa, but not all of them got there!
Look at the map below, and write sentences about what happened, like the models.

Tȟaté Wíŋ haŋp'íkčeka kšúpi kiŋ héna hóčhoka-ta aí šni.
Kȟaŋǧí waŋ haŋp'íkčeka kiŋ ikíču.

Nihíŋčiyapi šni yo. Kȟaŋǧí waŋ haŋp'íkčeka kiŋ ičú k'uŋ hé Míla Kič'úŋ ó. Na šúŋka kiŋ é na wičhítegleǧa kiŋ Tȟašúŋke Ská wičháo.

**14** Now let's try this in your classroom! First, your teacher will show you some pictures or things. Next, close your eyes! When you open them, look around you. Somebody took some of the things to the center. Nobody took other things. Use the models to help write sentences about what happened.

> Tuwá (haŋp'íkčeka kiŋ) hóčhoka-ta aí.
> Tuwéni (haŋp'íkčeka kiŋ) hóčhoka-ta aí šni.

**15** Skim through the first part of the dialogue below. Bob and the others are having Bob's naming ceremony. Skim through the dialogue. What name do they give Bob? Write it here: _____

Tȟašúŋke Ská: **Tȟuŋšká, wanáuŋsapi k'uŋ héhaŋ líla taŋyáŋ ečhánuŋ weló. Čha hé uŋ líla íuŋtaŋpe ló. Lakȟóta hokšíla heníčha, k'éyaš tȟokéya waŋúŋniyaŋkapi k'uŋ héhaŋ Lakȟól wičhóuŋ kiŋ taŋyáŋ slolyáye šni s'elé. Na wanáš wakhútepi uŋníspe. Ičhíŋ ptéȟčaka waŋ tȟokáheya yaó.**

Bob: **Waúŋspemayakhiyapi k'uŋ hená philámayayape ló.**

Tȟašúŋke Ská: **Ptéȟčaka waŋ tȟokáheya yaó k'uŋ hé uŋ čhaš'úŋnitȟuŋpi kte. Mičhíŋkši čhičáǧiŋ kte. Ho na letáŋhaŋ Wičhóȟ'aŋ Gloníča eyá čhaš'úŋnitȟuŋpi kte. Ȟesápa kiŋ lél čhažé kiŋ lé uŋníč'upi. Ȟesápa kiŋ lé Wakȟáŋ Tȟáŋka makȟá kiŋ lé čhokáŋyaŋ ahígnaka čha hé ikčé wičháša lél nážiŋpi kiŋ lená tȟáwape ló. Ho čha thiyáta yakhí kiŋháŋ Lakȟóta wičhóȟ'aŋ na wičhóuŋ nakíčižiŋ yo.**

Bob: **Lakȟól wičhóȟ'aŋ na wičhóuŋ kiŋ hená waníl áyiŋ kta wóinapȟeke. Ho čha tókhel okíhika nawéčižiŋ kte.**

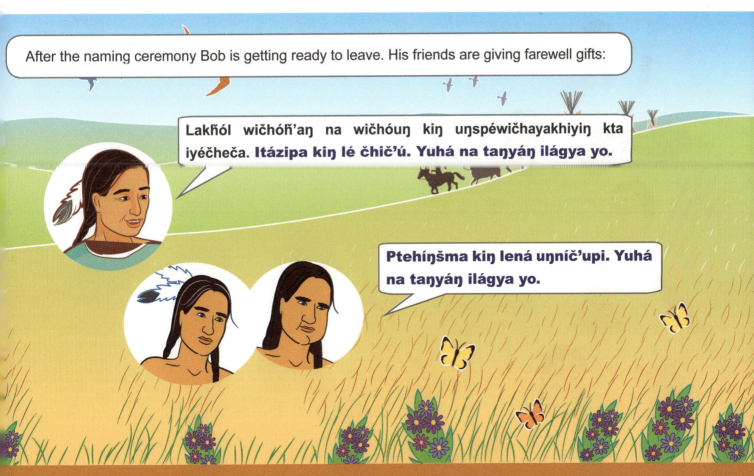

After the naming ceremony Bob is getting ready to leave. His friends are giving farewell gifts:

Lakȟól wičhóȟ'aŋ na wičhóuŋ kiŋ uŋspéwičhayakhiyiŋ kta iyéčheča. Itázipa kiŋ lé čhič'ú. Yuhá na taŋyáŋ ilágya yo.

Ptehíŋšma kiŋ lená uŋníč'upi. Yuhá na taŋyáŋ ilágya yo.

**16** Read through the first part of the dialogue again, and circle the best ending for each sentence.

1. Bob tȟokéya Lakȟóta wičhóthi-ta í k'uŋ héhaŋ...
   a. Bob Lakȟól wičhóuŋ kiŋ taŋyáŋ slolyé šni.
   b. Bob Lakȟól wičhóuŋ kiŋ taŋyáŋ slolyé.
   č. Bob ptéȟčaka waŋ tȟaŋníš ó.

2. Bob Lakȟóta wičhóthi kiŋ él úŋ k'uŋ ečhúŋhaŋ...
   a. ptéȟčaka tákuni ó šni.
   b. ptéȟčaka waŋžíla ó.
   č. ptéȟčaka óta wičháo.

3. Tȟokáheya ptéȟčaka waŋ ó k'uŋ hé uŋ...
   a. thiíkčeya waŋ k'úpi kte.
   b. čhažé k'úpi kte.
   č. šúŋkawakȟáŋ etáŋ wičhák'upi kte.

4. Tȟašúŋke Ská Bob...
   a. čhiyéku káǧiŋ kte.
   b. lekšítku káǧiŋ kte.
   č. čhiŋkšítku káǧiŋ kte.

5. Bob thiyáta khí kiŋháŋ...
   a. pispíza kiŋ nawíčhakičižiŋ kte héčha.
   b. Lakȟól wičhóuŋ nakíčižiŋ kte héčha.
   č. Tȟaté Wiŋ nakíčižiŋ kte héčha.

6. Nakúŋš agná Bob thiyáta khí kiŋháŋ...
   a. wičhóuŋ kiŋ uŋspéwičhakhiyiŋ kta iyéčheča.
   b. Lakȟótiyapi uŋspéwičhakhiyiŋ kta iyéčheča.
   č. wašíčuiyapi uŋspéwičhakhiyiŋ kta iyéčheča.

**17** Look at the pictures, and look at the model sentences in blue, in the dialogue on page 109 in which Tȟašúŋke Ská gives Bob a bow, and some of the hunters give Bob buffalo robes. Then, fill in the rest of the speech bubbles for each gift.

**18** Skim through the frames of the following dialogue. Then read the questions and circle the best answer.

Bob thiyáta khí he? Naíŋš Lisa eháŋni wičhóthi-ta í he?

A) Bob thiyáta khí.

B) Lisa eháŋni wičhóthi-ta í.

Tȟuŋšká, akhé waŋúŋniyaŋkapi kte kiŋ slolwáye šni. Ho éyaš uŋkíksuya po. Ho na lé taŋyáŋ kiksúya yo: Óhiŋniyaŋ Lakȟól Wičhóȟ'aŋ kiŋ ognáúŋ na gluhá máni yo. Na gloníča yo.

Tóhaŋni éčhiktuŋžapi kte šni yeló. Wókiksuye óta mayák'upe ló. Na nakúŋ takúku óta uŋspémayakhiyapi na ablésmayayape ló. Ho čha líla philámayayape ló.

Bob! Ičhéwiŋš takúku óta ayáhi kštó. Lená tuwá nič'ú he? Táku tókȟa he?

Eháŋk'ehaŋ Lakȟóta kiŋ wanásapi čha él ówapȟa. Na ptéȟčaka waŋ tȟokáheya ȟčiŋ wakté. Na heháŋl Ȟé Sápa-takiya uŋyáŋpi na uŋkípi háŋl Lakȟól čhažé waŋ mak'úpe ló. Wičhóȟ'aŋ Gloníče eyá čhašmátȟuŋpi. Na heháŋl takúku óta mak'úpi. Wókiksuye eyá otúmakiȟ'aŋpi. Na niyé kȟó wókiksuye eyá hiyúničhiyape ló.

Wičhóȟ'aŋ Gloníče eyápi he? Ho čha ták tókȟanuŋ kta he?

Tókheškhe waȟ'áŋ kte kiŋ slolwákiye šni. Ho éyaš ithúšekaš iblútȟiŋ kte héčha. Lakȟól wičhóȟ'aŋ na wičhóuŋ kiŋ lená theȟíla-phiča. Čha takómni uŋglóničapi kte héčha. **Wáŋ lé wáŋ, itázipa waŋ Tȟašúŋke Ská mak'ú k'uŋ lé é. Čhaŋkȟóhaŋ waŋ Tȟaté-wiŋ húŋku kiŋ hiyúničhiya čha wáŋ lé wáŋ!**

**19** Can you finish the dialogue? Look at the model sentence in blue, and then write in what Bob would say for each gift he shows Lisa. (Hint: if you need some help, look at exercise 11 on page 107).

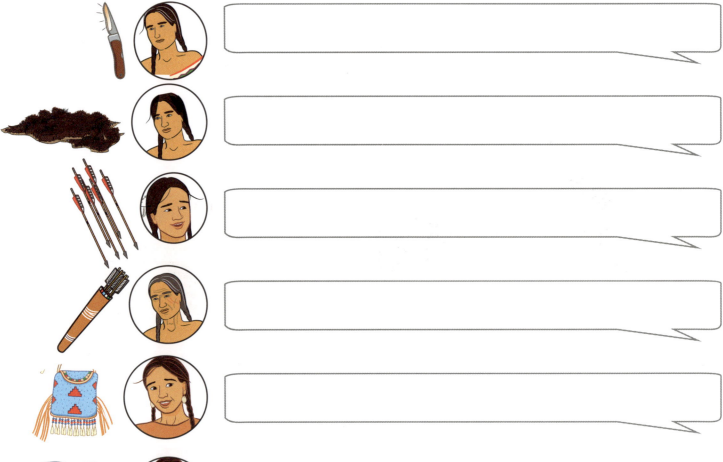

Čhaŋkȟóhaŋ waŋ Tȟaté-wiŋ húŋku kiŋ hiyúničhiya čha lé é.

**20** Tȟašúŋke Ská táku Bob kiksúye-ší he?

a) Lakȟól wičhóȟ'aŋ kiŋ kiksúye-ší.

b) Lakȟóta kiŋ tókhel wanásapi k'uŋ hé kiksúye-ší.

č) Haŋp'íkčeka kiŋ tuktél ékignakiŋ kta héči hé kiksúye-ší.

Níš-eyá Lakȟól'iyapi na Lakȟól wičhóuŋ kiŋ óhiŋniyaŋ kiksúyapi na gluhá máni po!

**áble - azíl'uŋyaŋpi**

**áble**  I am taking it there, see **áyA**

**ablésmayayape**  you made me notice it/him/her, see **ablésyA**

**ablésyA**  to make one notice something

**ablézA**  to notice or realize smth

**ačháŋzekA**  to be angry with someone

**ačhíyuptapi**  see **ayúptA**

**ačhíyuptiŋ**  see **ayúptA**

**ačhíyuta**  see **ayúta**

**ačhíyutapi**  see **ayúta**

**aglágla**  alongside smth, along the side of

**aglí**  to bring smth/sb back

**agná**  moreover

**ahí**  to bring smth/sb

**aȟíčahAŋ**  to trip on smth and fall

**ahígnakA**  to bring smth and lay it down

**ahíyaya**  to sing smth

**aí**  to transport/take smth/sb there (having arrived there)

**aígluštaŋ**  to let oneself go all out in smth

**aíȟat'A**  to laugh at sb

**aínab**  on the farther side of smth

**akáŋl**  on/upon smth

**akáŋlkaŋl**  on/upon more than one thing

**akáŋwaeglepi**  a shelf

**akáŋwowapi**  a desk

**akáŋyaŋkA**  to ride on smth

**akéwaŋži**  eleven

**akhé**  again

**akhéšna**  habitually again

**akhíčaškA**  to tie smth to or on, tie together

**akhígle**  times (with numerals)

**akhípȟa**  for smth to happen to one, to experience smth

**akȟótaŋhaŋ**  from or on the other side of smth

**akíčhita**  soldier

**akíčhiyapi**  to compete with each other, to contest with each other

**alí**  to step on smth/sb

**alúpta**  see **ayúptA**

**amáyaluptiŋ**  see **ayúptA**

**amáyaluta**  see **ayúta**

**amáye**  see **áyA**

**ámniŋ**  see **áyA**

**anáǧoptaŋ**  to listen to smth/sb

**anátaŋ**  to make an attack on smth/sb

**anáuŋǧoptaŋpi**  see **anáǧoptaŋ**

**anáuŋniǧoptaŋpi**  see **anáǧoptaŋ**

**ániŋ**  see **áyA**

**aŋpétu**  day

**Aŋpétuwakȟáŋ**  Sunday

**aóhomniyaŋ**  around smth/sb

**aókawiŋȟ**  circling around sb/smth

**aópemni**  to wrap smth up in smth

**apȟá**  to hit smth/sb

**apȟé**  to wait for sb

**apsíčA**  to jump over smth/sb

**asáŋpi**  milk

**asáŋpi yuslí**  to milk

**asníkiya**  to take some rest

**áta**  completely

**átaya** [1]  completely

**átaya** [2]  to meet sb

**até**  my father

**aténiyaŋ**  see **atéyA**

**atéyA**  to have sb for father

**atkúku**  his/her father

**aú**  to be bringing smth/sb

**awábleze**  see **ablézA**

**awáhi**  see **ahí**

**awái**  see **aí**

**awáŋyaŋkA**  to look after smth/sb

**awáštelakA**  to like doing smth

**awášteyalakapi**  see **awáštelakA**

**awáu**  see **aú**

**awíčhahipi**  see **ahí**

**awíčhapȟe**  see **apȟá**

**awíčhawai**  see **aí**

**awíčhayuptapi**  see **ayúptA**

**áyA**  to be on the way taking smth/sb there

**ayábleza**  see **ablézA**

**ayáhi**  see **ahí**

**áyapi**  see **áyA**

**áye**  see **áyA**

**áyiŋ**  see **áyA**

**ayúptA**  to answer sb

**ayúta**  to look at sb/smth

**azíl'uŋyaŋpi**  see **azílyA**

# Glossary

azílwičhaye  see **azílyA**

azílyA  to smudge smth/sb

azíŋ  to nurse, to suck milk from a mother's breast

blaská  to be flat

blatké  see **yatkÁŋ**

blawá  see **yawá**

blažó  see **yažó**

blé [1]  lake

blé [2]  see **yÁ**

blihíč'iya  to take courage

bló  potato

bloká  male

blokéhaŋ  last summer

blokétu  summer

blopátȟaŋpi  mashed potatoes

blóza  pelican

bluhá  see **yuhá**

bluwíŋyeya  see **yuwíŋyeya**

blužáža  see **yužáža**

blúze  see pȟóskil **yúzA**

čépȟaŋšiwaye  see **čépȟaŋšiyA**

čépȟaŋšiyA  to have sb for a female cousin (female reference)

čha [1]  so, therefore

čha [2]  marks a relative clause

čhaŋ [1]  whenever - then, repeatedly during such time/event

čháŋ [2]  wood

čháŋ [3]  day, 24 hours

čhaŋáletka  branch

čháŋčheǧa  drum

čhaŋk'íŋ  to carry fuel wood

čhaŋkábu  to drum

čhaŋkázuŋtapi  backrest

čhaŋkȟóhaŋ  the parts along the backbone

čhaŋkȟóžuha  strike-a-light pouch

čhaŋksáyuha  policeman

čhaŋmáhel  in the woods

čhaŋmháŋska  candy

čháŋna  whenever/then, always during such time/event

čhaŋnúŋpa [1]  a pipe

čhaŋnúŋpa [2]  to smoke tobacco

čhaŋóphiye  a trunk, storage trunk, wooden box

čhaŋtéšičA  to be sad

čhaŋtéwašteya  happily

čháŋthipi  log house

čhaŋwák'iŋ  see **čhaŋk'íŋ**

čhaŋwákabu  see **čhaŋkábu**

čhaŋwákšiča  wooden dish/bowl

čhaŋyátaŋhaŋ  from the woods

čhaŋzékA  to be angry

čhápa  beaver

čhaš'úŋnitȟuŋpi  see **čhaštȟúŋ**

čhaš'úŋtȟuŋpi  see **čhaštȟúŋ**

čhašmátȟuŋpi  see **čhaštȟúŋ**

čhaštȟúŋ  to name sb/smth

čhatkúta  at the back of a tent or room

čhažé  his/her name

čhažéyatA  to call sb/smth by name

čhebčhépapi  see **čhépA**

čhéǧa  kettle, pot, pail, bucket

čhépA  to be fat/chubby

čhepčhépapi  see **čhépA**

čheslí  poop

čhetáŋ  hawk

čhethí  to make fire

čhéyA  to cry, weep

čhič'ú  see **k'ú**

čhič'úpi  see **k'ú**

čhičáǧiŋ  see **káǧA**; ('I will make you')

čhičáhi  see **kahí**

čhičípahi  see **pahí**

čhičípazopi  see **kipázo**

čhičíyuǧaŋ  see **kiyúǧaŋ**

čhičíyuȟpiŋ  see **kiyúȟpA**

čhičíyute  see **kiyútA**

čhíŋ  to want smth

čhiŋkší  my son

čhiŋkšítku  his/her son

čhiŋkšíyA  to have sb for a son

čhiŋtók  certainly, of course

čhiyéku  his older brother

čhiyéyA  to have sb for older brother (male reference)

čhiyúȟičapi  see **yuȟíčA**

čhiyúȟičiŋ  see **yuȟíčA**

čhokáŋgnagya  placing smth in the middle

**čhokáŋyaŋ** in the middle

**čhuŋkší** my daughter

**čhúŋšoke** forest, deep woods

**čhuwéku** her older sister

**čhuwí** back (body part)

**čhuwíč'iŋpa** cradleboard (carried on the back)

**čhuwígnaka** a dress

**čík'ala** to be small

**čónala** few, not many

**é** to be (identification to be the one)

**Ečéš!** expresses disapproval, doubt, disappointment, disbelief or surprise (used mostly by women)

**ečhámuŋ** see **ečhúŋ**

**ečhánuŋ** see **ečhúŋ**

**ečháŋni** soon, early

**ečhékčhe** see **ečhél**

**ečhél** in the right way, as it was originally, as it should be, as is normal or proper, properly

**ečhétkiya** in the direction of smth/sb

**ečhíčiye** see **ekíyA**

**éčhiktuŋžapi** see **éktuŋžA**

**ečhúŋ** to do smth

**ečhúŋhaŋ** in the meantime

**ečhúŋk'uŋpi** see **ečhúŋ**

**ečíyapi** to be called

**éeye** instead

**égle** to set/place smth (especially in a vertical position)

**égna** among

**égnakA** to set/place smth (especially in a horizontal position)

**eháke** last one

**ehákeȟčiŋ** finally

**eháŋk'ehaŋ** traditional, of the old days

**eháŋl** at that time in the past

**eháŋni** long ago

**ékignakA** to place smth for sb

**ekíyA** to say smth to sb

**ektá** at, to

**ektáni** back at, staying at

**éktuŋžA** to forget smth/sb

**él** in, at, to

**emáčiyapi** see **ečíyA** ('my name is')

**éna** staying in place

**eníčiyapi** see **ečíyA** ('your name is')

**épazo** to point at smth/sb there

**éslol'uŋyaŋpi** see **éslolyA**

**éslolyA** to go and find out about smth, go and learn about smth

**etáŋ** [1] from

**etáŋ** [2] some (plural hypothetical)

**etáŋhaŋ** from

**éthi** to go and make a camp

**étkiya** toward, in the direction of

**étuŋwAŋ** to look there (away from here)

**éuŋglepi** see **égle**

**éuŋgnakiŋ** see **égnakA**

**éuŋpA** to lay or place smth/sb

**éuŋthipi** see **éthi**

**éwagle** see **égle**

**éwagnakiŋ** see **égnakA**

**éwaktuŋža** see **éktuŋžA**

**éwaŋuŋyaŋka** see **éwaŋyaŋkA**

**éwaŋuŋyaŋkapi** see **éwaŋyaŋkA**

**éwaŋuŋyaŋkiŋ** see **éwaŋyaŋkA**

**éwaŋyaŋkA** to go and look at smth/sb

**éwauŋpe** see **éuŋpA**

**éwektuŋže** see **éktuŋžA**

**eyá** [1] well, er, so, uh

**eyÁ** [2] to say that (what is quoted)

**eyá** [3] some certain ones

**eyá** [4] too, also (as in **íŋš-eyá**)

**éyagnakapi** see **égnakA**

**eyápi** see **eyÁ**

**éyaš** but

**éyayA** they all left (as a group)

**éyokas'iŋ** to peek, to take a peek

**éyouŋkas'iŋ** see **éyokas'iŋ**

**ǧí** to be brown

**glÁ** to be on the way back there

**glakíŋyaŋ** transverse (not crosswise), transversely at right angles to

**glápi** see **glÁ**

**gleškÁ** to be spotted

**gleškáškapi** see **gleškÁ**

**glí** to have come back here

**gloníča** to refuse to give up one's own

# Glossary

**gluhá** to have smth/sb of one's own

**glušlókA** to pull off smth of one's own

**gluwíŋyeya** to make smth of one's own ready

**hÁŋ** to stand (of inanimate vertical things)

**háŋ** yes

**haŋhépi** night

**haŋkášiwaye** see **haŋkášiyA**

**haŋkášiyA** to have sb for a female cousin (male reference)

**haŋké** a part of

**haŋkéni** no part of

**haŋkéya** finally

**háŋl** at that specified time

**haŋní** see **šni haŋni**

**haŋp'íkčeka** moccasins

**háŋpa** shoe

**háŋpapȟečhuŋpi** moccasin game (today called hand game)

**haŋpí** juice of smth

**háŋskA** to be long or tall

**háŋskaska** see **háŋskA**

**háŋtaŋš** if (in the future)

**haótkeye** closet, wardrobe

**háš** Such bad luck! Heck! Shucks!

**hayápi** clothes

**hé** that

**he?** marks a question

**héčha** to be of such kind/class

**héčhel** in that way, thus

**héčhena** still, continuing

**héčhetu** it is so, it is correct, thus it happened

**héčhuŋ** to do that

**héčhuŋk'uŋ** see **héčhuŋ**

**héči** [1] marks a polite suggestion

**héči** [2] if it is already the case

**héhaŋ** see **k'uŋ héhaŋ**

**heháŋl** next after that

**heháŋtu** it was then

**hékta** back

**héktakiya** towards the rear

**hél** there

**hemáčha** see **héčha**

**hená** those

**henáos** those two

**heníčha** see **héčha**

**hetáŋhaŋ** from there

**hétu** it is there

**hí** [1] tooth

**hí** [2] to have come here

**hinápȟA** to come out

**hinážiŋ** to come and stand

**híŋ** [1] body hair, fur

**híŋ** [2] oops

**híŋ** [3] see **hÁŋ**

**hiŋglÁ** to suddenly happen/become

**híŋhaŋni** morning

**hiŋȟpáye** to fall

**hípi** see **hí**

**hiyá** no

**hiyáyA** to be passing by on the way there

**hiyú** to step forth

**hiyúčhičhiyiŋ** see **hiyúkhiyA**

**hiyúkhiyA** to send smth/sb from there to sb (toward here)

**hiyúmakhiya** see **hiyúkhiyA**

**hiyúničhiya** see **hiyúkhiyA**

**hiyúničhiyape** see **hiyúkhiyA**

**ho** well (sentence launching expression)

**hóčhoka** the center of the camp circle

**Hóȟ!** by men only; expresses denial/opposition to an expressed opinion

**hókahé** Let's do it!

**hokhúwa** to go fishing

**hokšíla** boy

**hoští** Tough! Too bad! Hard luck!

**hótȟaŋka** to have a loud voice

**hótȟaŋkiŋkiŋyaŋpi** see **hótȟaŋka**

**hoúŋkhuwa** see **hokhúwa**

**howákhuwa** see **hokhúwa**

**hú** leg

**huhú** bone, bones

**hunáhomnipi** bicycle

**huŋǧéni** no part of a group or mass, none of a group or mass

**húŋȟ** some, some of, a number of

**huŋhuŋhé** expresses a wide range of emotions (as pleasure, surprise, gratitude, disappointment) depending on the tone and context

**húŋkešni - íŋš**

**húŋkešni** to be weak

**Húŋkpapȟa** one of the Lakota tribes

**húŋku** his/her mother

**hupáwaheyuŋpi** travois

**hušté** to be lame

**húte** the bottom part or the lowest part of smth

**hwo?** marks a question spoken by a man in a formal situation

**ȟčiŋ** really, very

**ȟé** mountain ridge

**Ȟé Sápa** Black Hills

**Ȟesápa** Black Hills

**ȟeyáb** away

**ȟpáyA** to lie, to be in a reclining position, to be lying

**ȟtálehaŋ** yesterday

**ȟtawáyata** see **ȟtawótA**

**ȟtawótA** to eat the evening meal, eat dinner, have dinner

**ȟtayétu** evening

**ȟupákiglake** bat

**ȟwá** to be sleepy

**ȟ'áŋ** to do

**ȟ'aŋhí** to be slow

**í** ¹ to have arrived there, to have been there

**í** ² mouth

**iblútȟiŋ** see **iyútȟA**

**ičábu** drum stick

**íčaŋyaŋ** leaning against smth

**íčáptaŋptaŋ kič'úŋ** to flip or turn over, to roll

**íčat'a** intensely, very much

**ičháǧA** to grow

**ičháŋtemawašte** see **ičháŋtewašte**

**ičháŋtewašte** to be glad because of smth

**ičhéwiŋš** how very!

**ičhéwiŋškaš** how very!

**ičhíčiču** see **ikíču**

**ičhíŋ** because, for

**ičínuŋpa** second, the second one

**ičítopa** fourth

**ičíyamni** third

**ičú** to take smth/sb

**iglág** moving camp, migrating

**iglákA** to move camp

**iglúštaŋ** to finish or complete smth pertaining to oneself, to be through

**iglúwiŋyeya** to prepare oneself, get ready

**iglúzA** to dress in a specified way

**igmú** cat

**igní** to search for smth

**iǧúǧa** rock

**ihákab** after smth, behind, following sb

**iháŋble** to dream about smth/sb

**iháŋke** the end of smth

**Iháŋktȟuŋwaŋna** the Yanktonai tribe

**iȟpéyA** to throw smth/sb down or away

**íiputȟakA** to kiss sb

**ikčé wičháša** native people, aboriginal people

**ikčéya** just, merely

**ikȟáŋčhola** radio

**ikhíyela** near to smth/sb

**ikíču** to take smth belonging to sb, take something for sb

**ikíkču** to take one's own

**íkimna** to consider sb the most capable or competitive in regard to smth, have confidence in another's efficiency, admire sb for his/her skills

**ikpáptaŋptaŋ** to roll over

**iktómi** spider

**Iktómi** Spider, the trickster of Lakota myths

**ilágyA** to make use of smth

**ilála** see **iyáyA**

**ilázata** behind smth/sb

**iléyA** to set fire on smth

**ilúkčaŋ** see **iyúkčaŋ**

**imáčhaǧe** see **ičháǧA**

**imákiču** see **ikíču**

**ímapuze** see **ípuzA**

**imáyaye** see **iyáyA**

**imúŋǧiŋ** see **iyúŋǧA**

**iná** my mother

**ináȟni** to hurry

**iníčhaǧe** see **ičháǧA**

**iníhaŋšni** disregarding, indifferently, paying no attention, not heeding,

**iníkaǧA** to make a sweatlodge ceremony

**iníuŋkaǧapi** see **iníkaǧA**

**inúŋka** see **iyúŋkA**

**íŋš** as for him/her/it

# Glossary

**íŋš-eyá**  he/she/it too

**íŋska**  expression of hesitancy

**íŋyaŋ**  stone

**íŋyaŋg**  running

**íŋyaŋkA**  to run

**íŋyaŋša**  sacred red pipe stone, so called Catlinite

**Íŋyaŋša Oók'e**  the quarry at Pipestone, MN, (lit.: red stone quarry)

**ipáhiŋ**  a pillow

**ipásisA**  to pin smth on smth, pin together, fasten with pins

**iphíyakA**  a belt

**ípi**  see **í**

**ípuzA**  to be thirsty

**ípuzapi**  see **ípuzA**

**ípuze**  see **ípuzA**

**isákhib**  next to

**isáŋm**  more than, over

**isáŋp**  more than, over

**išnála**  he/she/it alone

**išníkal éš**  (of relief) Luckily!

**ištámaza**  glasses

**ištíŋmA**  to sleep

**ítaŋ**  to be proud

**itázipa**  a bow (weapon)

**ité**  his/her face

**itéšniyaŋ**  really, seriously

**itȟáŋčhaŋ**  chief

**itȟáŋčhaŋyaŋpi**  they have him for a chief

**itȟáŋkal**  outside of smth

**itȟíčhičaške**  tripod (when setting up a tipi)

**itȟó**  let me ...

**itȟókab**  before smth (space and time)

**ithúšekaš**  in spite of everything, despite the struggle, at all costs, by all means

**itókaǧataŋhaŋ**  from the south; on the south side of, to the south of

**itówa**  to draw a picture of smth/sb

**itówapi**  a picture

**itóyawa**  see **itówa**

**íuŋkiputȟakapi**  see **íiputȟakA**

**íuŋtaŋpe**  see **ítaŋ**

**iwáču**  see **ičú**

**iwátȟokšu**  truck

**iwíčhaču**  see **ičú**

**iyÁ**  to speak, speak a language

**iyáču**  see **ičú**

**iyáwapi**  to count or calculate smth

**iyáyA**  to leave here, to set off from here, to have gone

**iyé** [1]  to be the one

**iyé** [2]  see **iyÁ**

**iyéčheča**  to be like smth/sb

**iyéčhel**  like smth/sb, in the same way as smth/sb

**iyéčhetu**  to happen as smth, be as smth/sb; become as smth (as mentioned), come true (as smth mentioned)

**iyéčhiŋkiŋyaŋke**  a car

**iyéčhiŋkyaŋka aphíye**  auto mechanic

**iyéčhiŋkyaŋke**  a car

**iyékiyA**  to recognize smth

**iyéuŋyaŋpi**  see **iyéyA**

**iyéuŋyiŋ**  see **iyéyA**

**iyéwaya**  see **iyéyA**

**iyéwičhuŋyaŋpi**  see **iyéyA**

**iyéyA**  to find smth/sb

**iyóhi**  to reach smth

**iyóhila**  each, every

**iyóȟlathe**  under smth

**íyokhihAŋ**  to be next in order/line to sb/smth, to stand next to

**iyókiphi**  to be pleased with smth/sb

**iyókišičA**  to be sad about, be unhappy with

**iyómakiphi**  see **iyókiphi**

**iyómakišiče**  see **iyókišičA**

**iyópteya**  straight on, passing on/by

**íyotakA**  to sit down

**iyówahi**  see **iyóhi**

**iyúha**  all

**iyúkčaŋ**  to be thinking about smth (in terms of forming one's opinion)

**iyúŋǧA**  to ask sb if smth is the case

**iyúŋkA**  to go to bed, to lie down

**iyúškiŋyaŋ**  happily, gladly

**iyúšloke**  key

**iyútȟA**  to try smth

**iyúwi**  to bind smth with smth

**k'éya**  see **má k'éya** and **wáŋ k'éya**

**k'éyaš - kšúpi**

k'éyaš  but

k'íŋ  to carry smth/sb

k'ú  to give smth to sb

k'uŋ  the aforementioned

k'uŋ héhaŋ  at that specified time

k'úpi  see **k'ú**

ká [1]  that one away from you and me

ka [2]  rhetorical question

ka [3]  strong negation

kaáyA  to take smth/sb there for sb

kablá  to jerk smth (as meat), cut thin for drying

káǧA  to make smth

kaǧéǧe  to sew or stitch smth

káǧiŋ  see **káǧA**

kaȟápA  to drive smth

kahí  to bring smth to sb

kaíyuzeya  at a distance, somewhat remote

kaíyuzeyakel  at a distance, somewhat remote

kákhiya  in that direction away from you and me

kál  there (away from you and me)

kasnásna  the rustling sound of falling leaves

kasótA  to wipe smth/sb out by striking (as killing people in war)

kaú  to be bringing smth/sb to sb

kaúŋspe  to train smth/sb (as a horse)

kazó  to draw a line

kečháŋmi  I think that, see **kéčhiŋ**

kéčhiŋ  to think that (about the thing or person in question)

kéyA  to say that (reported speech)

kȟaŋǧi  crow

kȟáŋta  plum

khéya  turtle

khí [1]  to have arrived returning there

khí [2]  to take away smth from sb

khiglÁ  to leave here in order to return back there

khigníŋ  see **khiglÁ**

khiíŋyaŋkA  to race

khilí  to be awesome, terrible, tough, good, cool; to be extreme/exceeding, be the limit

khípi  see **khí**

kȟó  too, also (refers to a noun)

kȟokȟóyaȟ'aŋla  chicken

kȟokípȟA  to fear smth/sb, be afraid of smth/sb

kȟoškálaka  young man

kȟoúŋkipȟapi  see **kȟokípȟA**

kȟoúŋničipȟapi  see **kȟokípȟA**

kȟowíčhakipȟa  see **kȟokípȟA**

khúl  downward

kȟúŋšitku  his/her grandmother

khuté  to shoot at smth/sb

khuwá  to chase smth/sb

kič'íŋ  to carry smth/sb of one's own on one's back

kič'úŋ  to use one's own, to put on or wear one's own

kíčaǧA  to make smth for sb

kíčala  to scatter smth pertaining to sb (of non-liquid material)

kičhí  with sb (only one person)

kičhízapi  they fight each other

kíčiyaŋkA  smth is there for sb

kignúŋg  diving, see **kignúŋkA**

kignúŋkA  to dive

kiksúyA  to remember smth/sb

kiktá  to get up, to wake up

kiníl  almost

kiŋ  the

kiŋháŋ  when ... then (future event)

kiŋyÁŋ  to fly

kiŋyékhiyapi  an airplane

kipáhi  to pick smth up for sb

kipápsuŋ  to spill smth belonging to sb

kipázo  to show smth to sb

kisúŋ  to braid one's own (as hair)

kitáŋla  a little, in a slight degree

kiúŋ  to use smth belonging to sb

kiyúǧaŋ  to open smth for sb

kiyúȟpA  to take smth down for sb

kiyúšičA  to spoil smth belonging to sb

kiyúsotA  to spend smth belonging to sb

kiyútA  to eat smth belonging to sb

kiyúweǧA  to break smth belonging to sb

kpaŋwáye  see **kpaŋyÁŋ**

kpaŋyÁŋ  to tan smth (as a hide)

ksápA  to be wise, smart

kštó  indicates assertion or emphasis

kšú  to bead smth

kšúpi  they bead, it is beaded

# Glossary

**kta**  will, would (indicates a potential - not yet real - action or state, often corresponds with English future tense)

**kte**  see **ktA**

**kté**  to kill smth/sb

**kú**  to be coming back

**lá** [1]  to ask for smth

**lá** [2]  see **yÁ**

**láŋ**  very

**lakȟáš**  evidently, must have (implies the idea of "because"), certainly, obviously

**Lakȟól**  Lakota, in Lakota way, of Lakota type

**Lakȟól'iyA**  to speak Lakota, speaking Lakota, in Lakota

**Lakȟól'iyapi**  the Lakota language

**Lakȟóta**  Lakota

**Lakȟótiyapi**  the Lakota language

**Lakȟótiyaye**  see **Lakȟól'iyA**

**lápi**  see **yÁ**

**lé** [1]  see **yÁ**

**lé** [2]  this

**lečhála**  new, recently

**lečhálake s'e**  recently

**léčhel**  this way

**léčhiya**  in this direction

**leháŋl**  nowadays, now, at this time

**lekší**  my uncle

**lekšítku**  his/her uncle

**lekšíwaya**  see **lekšíyA**

**lekšíyA**  to have sb for uncle

**lél**  here

**lená**  these

**letáŋhaŋ**  from here

**líla**  very

**ločhíŋ**  to be hungry

**lol'íȟ'aŋ**  to cook

**lowáčhiŋ**  see **ločhíŋ**

**lowáŋ**  to sing

**loyáčhiŋ**  see **ločhíŋ**

**luhá**  see **yuhá**

**lúta**  red, scarlet

**lúza**  see **pȟóskil yúzA**

**lúzahAŋ**  to be swift or fast in running, fleet-footed

**lúzahe**  see **lúzahAŋ**

**má k'éya**  Ridiculous! Nonsense! Foolish! Don't you know!

(used by females)

**mahél**  inside

**maŋpíya**  cloud, sky

**mak'ú**  see **k'ú**

**mak'úpe**  see **k'ú**

**mak'úpi**  see **k'ú**

**makȟá**  earth, ground

**makȟásitomniyaŋ**  all over the world, everywhere in the world

**makhínapte**  spade

**makȟóčhe**  country

**makípahi**  see **kipáhi**

**makípazo**  see **kipázo**

**makíyuǧaŋ**  see **kiyúǧaŋ**

**makíyuȟpa**  see **kiyúȟpA**

**makíyusote**  see **kiyúsotA**

**máni**  to walk

**máni-khiya**  to let sb/smth walk, to walk sb/smth

**maŋkíŋ**  see **yaŋkÁ**

**mas'ákipȟA**  to call sb on the phone

**mas'ápȟA**  to make a phone call

**mas'áuŋkipȟapi**  see **mas'ákipȟA**

**mas'áuŋničipȟapi**  see **mas'ákipȟA**

**mas'íyapȟe**  see **mas'ápȟA**

**mas'íyužipe**  pliers

**mas'óčhethi**  stove

**mas'óphiye**  store, shop

**mastáke**  see **stákA**

**maštíŋča**  rabbit

**Maštíŋča Oyáte**  The Cree

**maštíŋčala**  rabbit

**maštíŋska**  rabbit

**maswógnaka**  can, tin

**matȟó**  bear

**matȟúŋpi**  I was born, see **tȟúŋpi**

**maúŋnipi**  see **máni**

**mayák'u**  see **k'ú**

**mayák'upe**  see **k'ú**

**mayákahi**  see **kahí**

**mayákipazo**  see **kipázo**

**mayáluȟičiŋ**  see **yuȟíčA**

**mazáptaŋ**  see **záptaŋ**

**mázaska**  money, dollar

**mícaǧe - ó**

**mícaǧe**  see **kícaǧA**

**mičhíŋkši**  my son

**míčiyaŋka**  see **kíčiyaŋkA**

**mihákab**  see **ihákab**

**míla**  knife

**míš**  I

**misákhib**  see **isákhib**

**míš-eyá**  me too

**mišnála**  I alone

**mitákuyepi**  my relatives

**mitȟá-**  my

**mitȟákoža**  my grandchild

**mitȟáwa**  my

**miyé**  I

**míyožuha**  knife case, knife-sheath

**mní**  water

**mníčiyapi**  they gather for a meeting

**mnikápȟopapi**  pop

**Mnilúzahe Otȟúŋwahe**  Rapid City, SD

**mnimíčiyapi**  see **mníčiyapi**

**mníŋ**  see **yÁ**

**mníógnake**  a water container

**mni-yátkaŋ**  to drink water

**na**  and

**na!**  indicates an informal command spoken by a woman

**naȟ'úŋ**  to hear smth/sb

**naháŋ**  and

**naháŋȟčiŋ**  still, yet, not yet

**naȟmála**  secretly, slyly, privately

**naȟtákA**  to kick smth/sb

**naíč'ižiŋ**  to defend oneself

**naíŋš**  or

**nakéš**  finally

**nakíčižiŋ**  to defend smth/sb

**nakpá**  external ear

**nakúŋ**  also (refers to an activity)

**nakúŋš**  also indeed, see **nakúŋ**

**napčíyuŋka**  nine

**napé**  his/her hand

**napéuŋniyuzapi**  see **napéyuzA**

**napéyuzA**  to shake sb's hand

**napȟÁ**  to flee, to run, run off, run away, retreat

**natáŋ**  to rush in to attack, to make a charge or an attack, to dash

**naúŋȟ'uŋpi**  see **naȟ'úŋ**

**naúŋȟtakapi**  see **naȟtákA**

**naúŋkič'ižiŋpi**  see **naíč'ižiŋ**

**naúŋniȟtakapi**  see **naȟtákA**

**nawáȟ'uŋ**  see **naȟ'úŋ**

**nawéčižiŋ**  see **nakíčižiŋ**

**nawíčhakičižiŋ**  see **nakíčižiŋ**

**nayáȟ'uŋ**  see **naȟ'úŋ**

**nayážiŋ**  see **nážiŋ**

**nayážiŋpi**  see **nážiŋ**

**nážiŋ**  to stand

**nazúŋspe**  an ax

**nič'ú**  see **k'ú**

**nič'ú**  see **k'ú**

**níčaǧa**  see **kíčaǧA**

**ničhíye**  your older brother (male reference), see **čhiyé**

**ničíyuȟpa**  see **kiyúȟpA**

**niglúze**  see **iglúzA**

**niȟ'áŋhipe**  see **ȟ'aŋhí**

**nihíŋčiyA**  to be frightened, scared, to panic

**nihíŋčiyemayaye**  see **nihíŋčiyeyA**

**nihíŋčiyewaye**  see **nihíŋčiyeyA**

**nihíŋčiyeyA**  to make sb frightened, scared

**nihiŋmíčiye**  see **nihíŋčiyA**

**nihúŋ**  your mother

**nikhílipe**  see **khilí**

**nikȟúŋši**  your grandmother

**níŋ**  see **yÁ**

**níš**  you

**níš-eyá**  you too

**nitȟá-**  your

**nitȟákȟola**  your friend (male reference)

**nitȟámaške**  your friend (female reference)

**nitȟáwa**  your

**nitȟúŋpi**  you were born, see **tȟúŋpi**

**nitúwe**  see **tuwé**

**niyé**  you

**núŋ**  see **úŋ**

**núŋm**  two

**núŋpa**  two

**nuŋwÁŋ**  to swim

**ó**  to hit smth/sb when shooting

# Glossary

**oákaŋke** chair

**oáli** a ladder

**oásnikiye** living room

**ób** with sb (more than one)

**obláye** a plain, flat land or place, meadow, prairie

**očháštȟuŋkA** to be famous, well known

**očhéthi** fire pit, a fireplace

**óčhičiyapi** see **ókiyA**

**óčhičiye** see **ókiyA**

**óčhičiyiŋ** see **ókiyA**

**očhíŋšičA** to be bad-tempered, ill-disposed; mean, irritable

**očhósya** being warm and comfortable, warmly, comfortably, cozily, snugly

**óǧeya** altogether, the whole thing, completely

**Oglála** Oglala

**ógle** shirt

**ogná** in, into; according to

**oȟ'áŋwašte** to have a pleasant personality or behavior, be kind, generous

**oháŋ** [1] alright, okay, ok

**ohÁŋ** [2] to wear smth on the foot

**ohíŋ** see **ohÁŋ**

**óhiŋniyaŋ** always

**ohítikA** to be brave, fierce, daring, furious, bold, foolhardy

**ohíyA** to win

**oȟláthe** underneath

**ohómni** around smth/sb

**ohómniyaŋ** around smth/sb

**oȟpáye** bedroom

**oíč'uŋnil hiŋglÁ** to give up, to be frozen into inaction (also **úŋč'uŋnil**)

**oíglakA** talk about oneself, tell one's own name, give one's background

**oíglužaža** bathroom

**oínažiŋ** station, see **wígli oínažiŋ**

**ok'Á** to dig smth

**okátaŋ** to stake smth

**okhížata** the forked end of smth, a fork in smth

**okhúl-waštépi** they are easy to shoot

**okíčhize** battle

**okíhi** can, be able to

**okíhika** see **tókhel okíhika**

**ókiyA** to help sb

**okíyakA** to tell sb smth

**okó** week

**okóihaŋke** weekend

**ól'ota** many in each case

**olé** to look for smth

**olól'iȟ'aŋ** kitchen

**olówaŋ** a song

**ómakiya** see **ókiyA**

**ománi** to travel, walk about

**ómapȟa** see **ópȟa**

**omás'apȟela** cell phone

**omáwani** see **ománi**

**ómayakiyiŋ** see **ókiyA**

**omníča** beans

**omníča yužápi** chili

**onáȟ'uŋ** to hear about smth/sb

**onákasni wičháša/wíŋyaŋ** fire fighter

**óničiya** see **ókiyA**

**oówaŋyaŋg wašté** to be good looking

**opápuŋ** outer edge

**opémni** to wrap smth/sb in

**ópȟa** [1] to be a member of

**ópȟa** [2] to take part in

**opȟétȟuŋ** to buy smth

**opȟéuŋtȟuŋ** see **opȟétȟuŋ**

**opȟéuŋtȟuŋpi** see **opȟétȟuŋ**

**opȟéwatȟuŋ** see **opȟétȟuŋ**

**opȟéyatȟuŋ** see **opȟétȟuŋ**

**opȟéyatȟuŋpi** see **opȟétȟuŋ**

**ophíye** box, container

**ópi** to be wounded; see **ó**

**ópta** through, across, over

**ósmaka** coulee, ravine, valley

**osnáze** a scar

**óštaŋ** to fit smth into smth

**oštékA** to be peculiar, queer, weird

**oštéštekA** see **oštékA**

**óta** many, a lot

**othéȟikA** to be expensive, to be a hardship

**othí** see **pteyúha othí**

**otȟúŋwahe** town

**otkÁ** smth is hanging

otkéwayiŋ  see otkéyA

otkéyA  to hang smth up

otkéyaye  see otkéyA

otúkiň'aŋ  to give smth to sb, to present or donate smth to sb

otúmakiň'aŋpi  see otúkiň'aŋ

otúwakiň'aŋ  see otúkiň'aŋ

óuŋkiyapi  see ókiyA

óuŋničiyapi  see ókiyA

óuŋyakiyapi  see ókiyA

owá  to write smth

owáhe  see ohÁŋ

owáhiŋ  see ohÁŋ

owákihi  see okíhi

owákšiyužaža  kitchen sink

owále  see olé

Owáŋkayužažapi  Saturday

ówapȟa  see ópȟa

owápȟe  hour

owáštečakA  a pleasant weather, pleasant place

owáyawa  school

owékinaháŋš  might, may, perhaps, possibly; there is a chance

ówičhuŋkiya  see ókiyA

ówičhuŋkiyiŋ  see ókiyA

ówiňaya  in a funny way

owíŋ  earrings

owíŋla  earrings

owíŋža  blanket

owóhiŋsko  taking one's own sweet time

owóte  dining room

owóte thípi  restaurant

oyákA  to tell smth, relate smth, tell on/about smth/sb

oyákihi  see okíhi

oyále  see olé

oyáŋke itȟáŋčhaŋ  tribal president

óyapȟa  see ópȟa

oyáte  people, tribe

oyúblaye  a page

oyúǧaŋ šíčA  it is difficult to open

oyúl šíčA  it tastes bad

oyúŋke  bed

oyúspA  to catch or grasp smth/sb

ožáŋžaŋglepi  window

pahá  hill

pahí  to pick smth

paílepi  flashlight

paŋȟyá  a lot, whole bunch, a heap

pápa  dried jerked meat, jerky

pasí  to research smth, make a study of, examine

pasnúŋ  to roast smth on a spit or stick

patȟáŋkal  pushing smth/sb outside/outdoors

patȟáŋktȟaŋkal  see patȟáŋkal

pawáŋkal  pushing smth upwards

pawóslal  pushing smth upward into a perpendicular position, erecting

pawóslaslal  see pawóslal

pe  indicates a command given by a woman to two or more people

pȟahíŋ  porcupine

pȟaŋǧí-zizí  carrot

pȟé  sharp

Pȟečhókaŋ Háŋska  Chinese

pȟégnaka  to wear smth in the hair (as a feather or an ornament)

pȟehíŋ  hair

pȟepȟé  see pȟé

pȟetížaŋžaŋ  lamp, light

pȟeží  grass

pȟežíȟota  sage

philámayayape  thank you (said to two or more people)

philámayaye  thank you (said to one person)

phiŋkpa  the top of anything, the tip, very end of the tip

pȟoǧó wičháša/wíŋyaŋ  council man/woman

pȟóskil yúzA  to hug sb

pispíza  prairie dog

po  indicates a command spoken by a man to two or more people

psíčA  to jump

psíŋ  rice

pšitȟó  beads

ptéčela  short

pteȟá  buffalo hide

ptéȟčaka  buffalo (generic term)

ptehíŋčala  buffalo calf

ptehíŋšma  buffalo hide with fur on it

# Glossary

**Ptesáŋ Wiŋ**  White Buffalo Woman

**ptewániyaŋpi**  cattle

**pteyúha othí**  ranch

**puswáye**  see **pusyÁ**

**pusyÁ**  to dry smth

**s'a**  habitually, regularly, often

**s'e**  as if

**s'elé**  it feels like, seems like

**s'eléčheča**  it feels like, seems like

**s'elél**  it feels like, seems like

**šá**  to be red

**šabkhíyA**  to make dirty smth belonging to sb

**šabšápe**  see **šápA**

**šaglóǧaŋ**  eight

**Šahíyela**  Cheyenne

**šakíyA**  to paint red smth of one's own

**šakówiŋ**  seven

**sáŋm**  more

**sápA**  to be black

**šápA**  to be dirty

**šapšápiŋ**  see **šápA**

**šašá**  see **šá**

**sáta**  horizontally placed pole or stick (used for hanging things on or for hanging a kettle over fire)

**Sčíli**  Pawnee, Skidi Pawnee (Skiri)

**séčA**  maybe, perhaps

**sél**  what if, I wonder, perhaps, possibly, it might be so (often expresses a rhetorical question)

**sí**  foot

**šíčA**  to be bad

**šináhiŋšma**  buffalo robe with fur

**siŋté**  its tail

**šiyótȟaŋka**  flute, whistle

**ská**  to be white

**škáŋ**  to stir, move about, be active, engaged in an activity, do things

**škaŋkápiŋ**  to be lazy, to be unwilling or reluctant to move about or stir

**škaŋškáŋ**  see **škáŋ**

**škaŋyákapiŋ**  see **škaŋkápiŋ**

**skaská**  see **ská**

**škátA**  to play

**škátiŋ**  see **škátA**

**škȟá**  in spite of, despite, but, and yet, nevertheless

**slol'úŋyaŋpi**  see **slolyÁ**

**slolkíyA**  to know one's own

**slolwákiye**  see **slolkíyA**

**slolwáye**  see **slolyÁ**

**slolyÁ**  to know smth/sb

**slolyáya**  see **slolyÁ**

**slolyáye**  see **slolyÁ**

**slolyé**  see **slolyÁ**

**šmá**  it is deep

**šna**  usually, habitually

**sní**  it is cold

**šni**  not

**šni haŋni**  before

**snisní**  see **sni**

**so**  marks conversational informal question, often used when the questioner does not expect an answer

**šókA**  to be thick (as cloth, board wood); dense (as woods); heavy (as cloth)

**stákA**  one's body part is tired or weary

**šuŋgmánitu**  coyote

**šuŋgsápa**  black horse

**šuŋȟpála**  puppy

**šuŋk'ákaŋmaŋkiŋ**  see **šuŋk'ákaŋyaŋkA**

**šuŋk'ákaŋnaŋkiŋ**  see **šuŋk'ákaŋyaŋkA**

**šuŋk'ákaŋuŋyaŋka**  see **šuŋk'ákaŋyaŋkA**

**šuŋk'ákaŋuŋyaŋkapi**  see **šuŋk'ákaŋyaŋkA**

**šuŋk'ákaŋuŋyaŋkiŋ**  see **šuŋk'ákaŋyaŋkA**

**šuŋk'ákaŋyaŋg**  see **šuŋk'ákaŋyaŋkA**

**šuŋk'ákaŋyaŋkA**  to ride horseback

**šúŋka**  dog

**šúŋkawakȟáŋ**  horse

**suŋkáyA**  to have sb for a younger brother

**šuŋksápa**  black horse

**sutá**  to be hard, solid, firm

**sutáya**  firmly, strongly

**tágni**  nothing

**ták**  see **táku**

**-takiya**  towards, in the direction of

**takómni**  certainly, it must be so

**táku**  what; something

**takúku**  various things, all sorts of things, whatever things

**tákuni**  nothing

## takúŋl - tȟogyé

takúŋl  something (potential)

tákuwe  why

-taŋhaŋ  from

taŋyáŋ  well; to be well; it is good that

taŋyéla  nicely, with precision, to perfection, completely, in a refined manner

tȟa-  his/her/its

tȟab'úŋškata  see **tȟabškátA**

tȟab'úŋškatapi  see **tȟabškátA**

tȟab'úŋškatiŋ  see **tȟabškátA**

tȟabškátA  to play basketball

tȟabškátapi  see **tȟabškátA**

tȟabwáškatiŋ  see **tȟabškátA**

tȟáȟca  deer

tȟáȟca-khuté  to hunt deer

tȟáȟca-khuwá  to chase deer

tȟaló  meat

tȟamáheča  to be

tȟaŋháŋši  my male cousin (male reference)

tȟaŋháŋšitku  his male cousin

tȟaŋíŋ  to be visible, to show, be obvious, appear

tȟáŋka  to be large, big

tȟaŋkál  outside

tȟaŋkátakiya  towards the outside

tȟaŋkátaŋhaŋ  from the outside

tȟaŋkíŋkiŋyaŋ  see **tȟáŋka**

tȟaŋkší  my younger sister (male reference)

tȟaŋnígnila  see **tȟaŋníla**

tȟaŋníš  already

tȟaŋpá  birch bark

tȟap'íčakȟape  baseball bat

tȟašína  her/his blanket

tȟaspáŋ  apple

tȟaspáŋhaŋpi  apple juice

tȟaspáŋpȟestola  pear

tȟašúŋke  his/her horse

tȟaté  wind

tȟatȟáŋka  buffalo bull

tȟatúye  direction, world quarter (as west, north, east, south)

tȟáwa  his/her/its

tȟawáčhiŋ  mind, reason; disposition; feeling; decision (in terms of one's inclination, opinion)

tȟáwape  their

tȟawówaši  his/her work

tȟeb'úŋyaŋpi  see **tȟebyÁ**

tȟebčhíčhiye  see **tȟebkhíyA**

tȟebkhíyA  to eat up smth that belongs to sb

tȟebwáye  see **tȟebyÁ**

tȟebyÁ  to consume smth by eating, eat smth up

tȟebyápi  see **tȟebyÁ**

tȟebyáya  see **tȟebyÁ**

tȟéhaŋ  for a long time

tȟéhaŋtu  it is far away

theȟíla  to love sb/smth, hold dear, cherish

theȟíla-phiča  it is to be loved and cherished

theníȟila  see **theȟíla**

theúŋȟilapi  see **theȟíla**

theúŋniȟilapi  see **theȟíla**

thí  to live (as in a place, area or house)

thiáphiyA  to fix/repair the house; to tidy/clean up the house/room

thibló  my older brother (female speaking)

thiblóku  her older brother

thihúȟaka  the poles of a tipi standing without the cover, the skeleton of a tent

thiíkčeya  tipi

thikáǧA  to set up a tipi, build a house

thimá  inside, in a house or tent

thimáhel  indoors

thimáhetaŋhaŋ  from indoors

thíŋpsiŋla  prairie turnip

thiókaȟmi  a corner of a room

thípi  house

thípi  they live, see **thí**

Thiská  White House

thiúŋkaǧapi  see **thikáǧA**

thiwáhe  family

thiwówaši  homework

thiyáta  at home

thiyóblečha  a tent

thiyópa  a door

thiyóšpaye  extended family group

tȟó  to be blue

tȟóéyaš  let me ..., first of all, give me a second

tȟogyé  differently, in a different way or manner

# Glossary

tȟóka   enemy

tȟoká   the first time, for the first time, at first (of time or space)

tȟokáheya   first

tȟokáta   in the future, later on, in the time to come

tȟokátakiya   in the future

tȟókča   to be different

tȟokéya   first, at first

tȟokíyA   to paint one's own blue

tȟoktȟókča   see tȟókča

tȟoška   my nephew (female reference)

tȟotȟó   see tȟó

tȟoyéla   in a blue condition, bluish (or greenish if talking about grass and leaves)

tȟožáŋ   my niece (female reference)

tȟózi   it is green

thukíha   shell (without the animal)

tȟuŋkášilawaya   see tȟuŋkášilayA

tȟuŋkášilayA   to have sb for grandfather

Tȟuŋkášilayapi   the US president

tȟuŋkášitku   his/her grandfather

tȟúŋpi   to be born

tȟuŋšká   my nephew (male reference)

tȟuŋškáyA   to have sb for a nephew (male reference)

tȟuŋwíŋ   my aunt

tȟuŋwíŋču   his/her aunt

thušú   tipi pole

tké   it is heavy

tketké   see tké

tkȟá   almost; but; used to, would have

tób   see tópa

tóhaŋ   when (in the past)

tóhaŋȟčiŋ   when, ever

tohánl   when (in the future or habitually)

tóhaŋni   never

tóhaŋyaŋ   how far, for how long

tók   how about it?

tók?   how about it?

tókča   what is it like?, there is something wrong with

tókȟa   smth is the matter, smth happens, smth is up, smth is wrong; to be in some kind of condition

tókȟaŋ'aŋ   to disappear

tókȟamaȟ'aŋ   see tókȟaȟ'aŋ

tókȟamuŋ   see tókȟuŋ

tókȟanuŋ   see tókȟuŋ

tokhé   expresses surprise (how can it be, isn't it); introduces a rhetorical question (I suppose, of course)

tókheča   to be some way or some kind; what is it like?, of what character is it? (also tókča)

tókhel   how

tókhel okíhika   as much as possible, as much as one is able to

tókheškhe   how

tókhi   where

tókhiya   where

tókȟuŋ   to do smth, do what

tókȟuŋk'uŋ   see tókȟuŋ

tókȟuŋk'uŋpi   see tókȟuŋ

tókȟuŋpi   see tókȟuŋ

tókša   surely (implies a promise to comply with a request in the future); eventually

tóktuka   to be some way, to be how, to happen in some way; how is it/he/she?

tomákča   see tókča

tóna   how many; several

tónakel   several

tónakiya   in several ways

tónapi   see toná

tópa   four, to be four

tuktél   where

tuktétaŋhaŋ   from where

tuŋwéya   a scout, a spy, a guide

tuwá   who

tuwé   to be who

tuwéni   no one

ú   to be coming

úŋ [1]   to be, to live

úŋ [2]   to use or wear smth

uŋ [3]   using, with, by means of

uŋ [4]   fast speech form of k'úŋ

uŋčhíŋpi   see čhíŋ

uŋčí   my grandmother

uŋčíwičhawaye   see uŋčíyA

uŋčíyA   to have sb for grandmother

uŋglóničapi   see gloníča

uŋglúhapi   see gluhá

uŋgná   maybe

**uŋgnáhela - uŋžíŋžiŋtka**

uŋgnáhela  suddenly
uŋgnáhelaka  suddenly
uŋgníŋ  see glÁ
uŋhípi  see hí
uŋk'úŋpi  see úŋ
uŋk'úpi  see k'ú
uŋk'úpi  see k'ú
uŋkáčhaŋzekapi  see ačháŋzekA
uŋkáǧapi  see káǧA
uŋkáhiyupi  see ahíyu
uŋkáiȟat'api  see aíȟat'A
uŋkáiniȟat'api  see aíȟat'A
uŋkánichaŋzekapi  see ačháŋzekA
uŋkánipȟapi  see apȟÁ
uŋkániyaŋpi  see áyA
uŋkápȟapi  see apȟÁ
uŋkápsičapi  see apsíčA
uŋkáupi  see kaú
uŋkáyaluptapi  see ayúptA
uŋkáyalutapi  see ayúta
uŋkáyapi  see áyA
uŋkáyuptapi  see ayúptA
uŋkáyutapi  see ayúta
uŋkhízapi  see khízA
uŋkhútepe  see khuté
uŋkhútepi  see khuté
uŋkhúwapi  see khuwá
uŋkíčaǧapi  see kíčaǧA
uŋkígluštaŋpi  see iglúštaŋ
uŋkígluwiŋyeyapi  see iglúwiŋyeya
uŋkíhakab  see ihákab
uŋkíkičupi  see ikíču
uŋkíkikčupi  see ikíkču
uŋkíksuya  see kiksúyA
uŋkíksuyapi  see kiksúyA
uŋkípazopi  see kipázo
uŋkípi  see í
uŋkíš  we
uŋkíš-eyá  we too
uŋkíyayapi  see iyáyA
uŋkíye  we
uŋkíyuŋǧiŋ  see iyúŋǧA
uŋkókihipi  see okíhi

uŋkóničhuwapi  see okhúwa
uŋkónilepi  see olé
uŋkóniyakapi  see okíyakA
uŋkópe  see ó
uŋkóyakapi  see oyákA
uŋkóyuspapi  see oyúspA
uŋkúŋspepi  see uŋspé
uŋmá  the other
uŋmáspe  see uŋspé
uŋníč'upi  see k'ú
uŋníč'upi  see k'ú
uŋníchizapi  see khízA
uŋníchutepi  see khuté
uŋníspe  see uŋspé
uŋníyaȟtakapi  see yaȟtákA
uŋnúŋwaŋpi  see nuŋwÁŋ
uŋnúŋwiŋ  see nuŋwÁŋ
úŋpi  see úŋ
uŋspé  to know how to do smth
uŋspéič'ičhiyA  to learn smth
uŋspékhiyA  to teach sb smth
uŋspémakhiyapi  see uŋspékhiyA
uŋspémayakhiyapi  see uŋspékhiyA
uŋspéničhiyiŋ  see uŋspékhiyA
uŋspéuŋkič'ičhiyapi  see uŋspéič'ičhiyA
uŋspéwičhakhiyiŋ  see uŋspékhiyA
uŋspéwičhayakhiyiŋ  see uŋspékhiyA
uŋspéwičhuŋkhiyapi  see uŋspékhiyA
uŋthípi  see thí
uŋyáhipi  see hí
uŋyáȟtakapi  see yaȟtákA
uŋyák'upi  see k'ú
uŋyákahipi  see kahí
uŋyáluȟičapi  see yuȟíčA
uŋyáŋkape  see yaŋkÁ
uŋyáŋkapi  see yaŋkÁ
uŋyáŋpi  see yÁ
uŋyíŋ  see yÁ
uŋyúȟičapi  see yuȟíčA
uŋyúonihaŋpi  see yuónihaŋ
uŋyútapi  see yútA
uŋyúzapi  see pȟóskil yúzA
uŋžíŋžiŋtka  tomato

# Glossary

uŋzóǧe  pants

waákhita  to be on the lookout, look around, scan about

wačhí  to dance

wačhípi  a dance; they dance; see **wačhí**

waglékšuŋ  turkey

waglí  see **glí**

waglúha  see **gluhá**

wáglutapi  table

wagmúšpaŋšni  watermelon

waȟ'áŋ  see **ȟ'áŋ**

wahí  see **hí**

wahínažiŋ  see **hinážiŋ**

waȟpé  leaf

waíŋmnaŋke  see **íŋyaŋkA**

wak'ú  see **k'ú**

wakábla  see **kablá**

wakáǧe  see **káǧA**

wakáǧeǧe  see **kaǧéǧe**

wakáǧeǧe  to sew things

wakȟáŋ  to be endowed with spiritual power, be sacred

wakȟáŋheža  child

wakhéya  tent

wakhéyaska  tent canvas

wakhí  see **khí**

wákhil  see **wákhita**

wákhita  to look around for things/people, be on the lookout, to be a guard

wakhúl  see **wakhúte**

wakhúte  to hunt

wakpá  river

wakpála  creek

wakšíča  plate, dish

wakšíškokpa  bowl

wakší-uŋyužažapi  see **wakšíyužaža**

wakšíyužaža  to wash dishes

wakšú  I beaded it

wakšú  to bead

wakšúpi  beading

waktá  to expect smth/sb, expect smth to happen, look forward to, look out,

wakté  see **kté**

wakú  see **kú**

waléǧa  bladder; bladder bag

wamátukȟa  see **watúkȟa**

wanáš  now indeed

wanásA  go for a buffalo hunt

wanáuŋsapi  see **wanásA**

waníča  there is none, it doesn't exist

wanil  see **waníčA**

waníyaŋpi  domestic animals, livestock

waníyetu  winter; year

waníyetu iyáwapi  winter count

wanúŋwiŋ  see **nuŋwÁŋ**

waŋ  a certain one

wáŋ k'éya!  Ridiculous! Nonsense! Foolish! Don't you know!? (used by males)

waŋ!  Look! Why! Here! Say! Gee! See! (used by males)

waŋbláka  see **waŋyáŋkA**

waŋbláke  see **waŋyáŋkA**

waŋblákiŋ  see **waŋyáŋkA**

waŋblí  eagle

wáŋčag  at once, immediately

wáŋčagna  at once, immediately, right away, instantly

waŋčhíyaŋkapi  see **waŋyáŋkA**

waŋčhíyaŋke  see **waŋyáŋkA**

waŋčhíyaŋkiŋ  see **waŋyáŋkA**

waŋglákA  to see one's own

waŋhíŋkpe  arrow

waŋláka  see **waŋyáŋkA**

waŋmáyalaka  see **waŋyáŋkA**

waŋná  now

waŋnáš  now indeed

waŋníyaŋg  see **waŋyáŋkA**

waŋníyaŋke  see **waŋyáŋkA**

waŋúŋniyaŋkapi  see **waŋyáŋkA**

waŋúŋyalakapi  see **waŋyáŋkA**

waŋúŋyaŋg  see **waŋyáŋkA**

waŋúŋyaŋkapi  see **waŋyáŋkA**

waŋwíčhablake  see **waŋyáŋkA**

waŋwíčhalaka  see **waŋyáŋkA**

waŋwíčhalakapi  see **waŋyáŋkA**

waŋwíčhayaŋkapi  see **waŋyáŋkA**

waŋwíčhayaŋke  see **waŋyáŋkA**

waŋyáŋg  see **waŋyáŋkA**

waŋyáŋkA  to see smth/sb

waŋyáŋkapi  see **waŋyáŋkA**

**waŋyáŋke- wičháša**

waŋyáŋke  see **waŋyáŋkA**

waŋyáŋkiŋ  see **waŋyáŋkA**

waŋyéglakiŋ  see **waŋglákA**

waŋží  a, any

waŋží  one

waŋžíla  only one

waŋžíni  no, none

wáŋžu  quiver

wapásnuŋ  see **pasnúŋ**

wapȟáha  war-bonnet; headdress with feathers

wapȟál  see **wapȟátA**

wapȟápȟa  to bark

wapȟátA  to butcher animals, do butchering

wapȟóštaŋ  hat

wapȟóštaŋla  cap

wašíču  white person

wašíčuiyA  to speak English

wašíčuiyapi  the English language

wašíŋska  bacon

waškátiŋ  see **škátA**

wasná  pemmican

wašté  to be good, pretty, beautiful

waštéčakA  to be kind

waštélakA  to like smth/sb

waštéšte  see **wašté**

waštéuŋlakapi  see **waštélakA**

waštéwičhalaka  see **waštélakA**

waštéyalaka  see **waštélakA**

wašúŋ  a den

wáta  see **yútA**

wáte  see **yútA**

wathí  see **thí**

watóhaŋl  when, sometime

watúkȟa  to be tired

waúŋ  see **úŋ**

waúŋkole  see **olé**

waúŋspekhiyA  to teach sb things

waúŋspemayakhiyapi  see **waúŋspekhiyA**

waúŋspewičhakhiya  see **waúŋspekhiyA**

waúŋspewičhakhiye  see **waúŋspekhiyA**

waúŋtukȟapi  see **watúkȟa**

waúŋyutapi  see **wótA**

waúŋyutiŋ  see **wótA**

wawákağeğe  see **wakáğeğe**

wawákšu  see **wakšú**

wawáŋyaŋg  see **wawáŋyaŋkA**

wawáŋyaŋkA  to see things/people, watch what is happening, observe

wawókiyA  to help people

wawóyakiyiŋ  see **wawókiyA**

wawóyuspa  policeman

wayáȟtakA  to bite people

wayášla  to graze

wayášlapi  see **wayášla**

wayátȟe-kuŋs  ruminating

wayátiŋ  see **wótA**

wayáwa  to study, to read things, to attend school

wayázaŋ  to be sick

wazí  pine

Wazí Aháŋhaŋ  Pine Ridge

wazíyatakiya  at/to the north

wazíyataŋhaŋ  from the north

we  indicates a command given by a woman to one person

wéč'iŋ  see **kič'íŋ**

wéksuye  see **kiksúyA**

wékta  see **kiktá**

weló  marks an assertion spoken by a man

wí  sun

wí mahél iyáyA  sun is setting down

wičákȟA  to tell the truth, to be right

wičála  to believe smth/sb, to agree to

wíčalu  a fan

wičáyakȟe  see **wičákȟA**

wíčazo  pen

wičháŋčala  old man

wičháŋpi  a star, stars

wičhák'upi  see **k'ú**

wičhákahi  see **kahí**

wičhákhutepi  see **khuté**

wičhákhuwa  see **khuwá**

wičhákhuwapi  see **khuwá**

wičhákte  see **kté**

wičháluha  see **yuhá**

wičháo  see **ó**

wičháopi  see **ó**

wičháša  man

# Glossary

**wičháyuhapi** see **yuhá**

**wičháyuonihaŋ** see **yuónihaŋ**

**wičhéška** front lacings of a tipi, the front of a tipi

**wičhéškipasise** tipi pins (for pinning together the front of the tipi)

**wičhíŋčala** girl

**wičhíteglega** racoon

**wičhítenaškaŋškaŋ** movie, television

**wičhóȟ'aŋ** custom, tradition, ceremony

**wičhóiye** word

**wičhóoyake** story

**wičhóthi** camp, village

**wičhóuŋ** a way of life

**wičhúŋkastopi** see **kasótA**

**wičhúŋkauŋspepi** see **kaúŋspe**

**wičhúŋkhutepi** see **khuté**

**wígli** oil

**wígli oínažiŋ** gas station

**wihúŋpaspa** tent pegs

**wihúta** base of a tipi, lower border of a tent

**wikčémna** ten

**wíkȟaŋ** rope

**wíkiyuŋ** to paint one's own

**winúȟčala** old woman

**wiŋčhíŋčala** girl

**wíŋyaŋ** woman

**wipȟá** tipi flaps, wind-flaps, the ears of a tipi

**wípȟe** weapon

**wiphípaha** the two poles holding up the tipi wind-flaps, flap poles

**wítaya** together, in company, in a group, gathered together

**wíuŋkiyuŋpi** see **wíkiyuŋ**

**wíwayuŋ** see **wíyuŋ**

**wíwičhayuŋ** see **wíyuŋ**

**wíwičhayuŋpi** see **wíyuŋ**

**wíwičhuŋyuŋpi** see **wíyuŋ**

**wíyaka** feather

**wíyapaȟiče** rear center pole (to which the tipi cover is tied and by which it is lifted onto the frame)

**wíyatke** a cup, drinking cup

**wiyóȟpeyata** at the west

**wiyóȟpeyatakiya** towards the west

**wiyóȟpeyataŋhaŋ** from the west

**wíyopȟewayiŋ** see **wíyopȟeyA**

**wíyopȟeyA** to sell smth/sb

**wíyopȟeye** see **wíyopȟeyA**

**wíyuhomni** screwdriver

**wíyuŋ** to paint smth

**wo** marks command spoken by a male

**wóableze** understanding, realization (of a fact)

**wóčhič'u** see **wók'u**

**wóčhič'upi** see **wók'u**

**wóglag** see **wóglakA**

**wóglakA** to speak, speak about things

**wóhela** a cook

**wóiȟakA** smth funny or laughable, a funny thing, a joke, a cause of laughter

**wóinapȟeke** danger, threat, smth that is dangerous, dangerous act or activity

**wók'u** to feed sb/smth

**wókȟokipȟe** to be dangerous, fearful, scary

**wókȟokipȟeke** to be dangerous, fearful, scary

**wókiksuye** an object to keep for memory,

**wókiyakA** to tell sb things, talk to, speak to sb

**wómayak'u** see **wók'u**

**wóphike** to be skillful in smth, talented, expert

**wóphila** thanks, gratitude, appreciation, gratefulness

**woslál** upright, perpendicularly, vertically

**wótA** to eat

**wótapi** see **wótA**

**wóte** see **wótA**

**wótȟaŋiŋ wówapi** newspaper

**wóuŋglakiŋ** see **wóglakA**

**wóuŋk'upi** see **wók'u**

**wóuŋničiyakapi** see **wókiyakA**

**wóuŋspe** lesson

**wóuŋyak'upi** see **wók'u**

**wówapi** book; letter

**wówapikağe** secretary

**wówaši** work

**wówaši káğA** to work

**wówičhak'u** see **wók'u**

**wówičhuŋk'upi** see **wók'u**

**wówiyuŋğe** a question

**wóyute** food

**wóžapi** traditional pudding

# Glossary

**wóžuha - zuzéča**

**wóžuha**  bag
**yÁ**  to go there
**yačhíŋ**  see **čhíŋ**
**yaglí**  see **glí**
**yahí**  see **hí**
**yaȟpáya**  see **ȟpáyA**
**yaȟtákA**  to bite smth/sb
**yaí**  see **í**
**yakáǧe**  see **káǧA**
**yakázo**  see **kazó**
**yakhí**  see **khí**
**yakú**  see **kú**
**yámni**  three
**yaŋkÁ**  to sit, be sitting
**yaŋkápi**  see **yaŋkÁ**
**yaŋké**  see **yaŋkÁ**
**yaó**  see **ó**
**yápi**  see **yÁ**
**yaškáŋ**  see **škáŋ**
**yasmí**  to make/pick smth bare with the mouth (as a bone)
**yathí**  see **thí**
**yatkÁŋ**  to drink smth
**yatkáŋpi**  see **yatkÁŋ**
**yaú**  see **ú**
**yaúŋ**  see **úŋ**
**yawá**  to read smth
**yawá-phiča**  it is to be read, it is good to read
**yažó**  to blow smth (as on an instrument), to play on (as a flute)
**ye**  indicates a command given by a woman to one person
**yé**  see **yÁ**
**yéksuyapi**  see **kiksúyA**
**yéksuye**  see **kiksúyA**
**yékta**  see **kiktá**
**yélakȟa!**  must have
**yeló**  assertion spoken by a man
**yetȟó**  familiar command spoken by a man, see nitȟó
**yíŋ**  see **yÁ**
**yo**  indicates a command given by a man to only one person
**yubláȟ**  pulling smth outstretched (as one's hands), pulling smth spreading it out or unfurling (as an umbrella, fan)
**yubláya**  to spread smth out flat with the hands, unfold, open out flat, lay out flat
**yuǧáŋ**  to open smth
**yuhá**  to have or keep smth
**yuhá-phiča**  it is good to have/keep
**yuhápi**  see **yuhá**
**yuȟíčA**  to wake sb up
**yukážal**  spreading smth apart
**yúl**  see **yútA**
**yunáyeyA**  to share what one obtained, to pass on smth received
**yuŋkȟáŋ**  and here, and then
**yuónihaŋ**  to honor sb
**yuósiŋyaŋ**  tied into a bow knot
**yuphíya**  nicely, finely
**yuš'íŋyeniye**  see **yuš'íŋyeyA**
**yuš'íŋyeuŋniyaŋpi**  see **yuš'íŋyeyA**
**yuš'íŋyeuŋyaŋpi**  see **yuš'íŋyeyA**
**yuš'íŋyeuŋyaŋpi**  see **yuš'íŋyeyA**
**yuš'íŋyeyA**  to surprise or startle sb
**yuslí**  see **asáŋpi yuslí**
**yut'íŋst'iŋza**  see **yut'íŋzA**
**yut'íŋzA**  to tighten smth (as a saddle-girth)
**yútA**  to eat smth
**yútiŋ**  see **yútA**
**yutítaŋ**  to pull smth
**yuwíŋyeya**  to prepare smth/sb, to get smth/sb ready
**yúzA**  to hold smth/sb, to take hold of smth/sb, to take up, seize, grab; see **phóskil yúzA**
**yužápi**  see **omníča yužápi**
**yužáža**  to wash smth/sb
**yuzíčA**  to stretch smth out by pulling, elongate, extend the length of smth
**yuzígzil**  see **yuzíčA**
**žaŋžáŋla**  to be transparent, translucent
**záptaŋ**  five
**zí**  to be yellow
**zičá**  squirrel
**zičáȟota**  gray squirrel (tree squirrel)
**ziŋtkála**  bird
**zíškopela**  banana
**zuzéča**  snake

Unit 1, Activity 16 (page 8)

Unit 2, Activity 12 (page 17)

**Unit 8, Activity 5 (page 68)**

**Unit 4, Activity 12 (page 34)**

**Partner One**

**Unit 6, Activity 6 (page 51)**

**Partner One**

**Unit 9, Activity 5a (page 79)**

**Partner One**

Here are Lisa's activities.

Lisa Saturday:        Lisa Sunday:

 9am  _____      10am _____

 1pm  _____      3pm  _____

 5pm  _____      7pm  _____

**Unit 4, Activity 12 (page 34)**

**Partner Two**

**Unit 6, Activity 6 (page 51)**

**Partner Two**

**Unit 9, Activity 5a (page 79)**

**Partner Two**

Here are Bob's activities.

Bob Saturday:     Bob Sunday:

 8am     9am

 10am     1pm

 3pm     8pm

Unit 5, Activity 13 (page 46)

**Unit 9, Activity 5b (page 79)**

Unit 9, Activity 6 (page 80)

 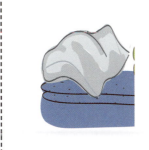  

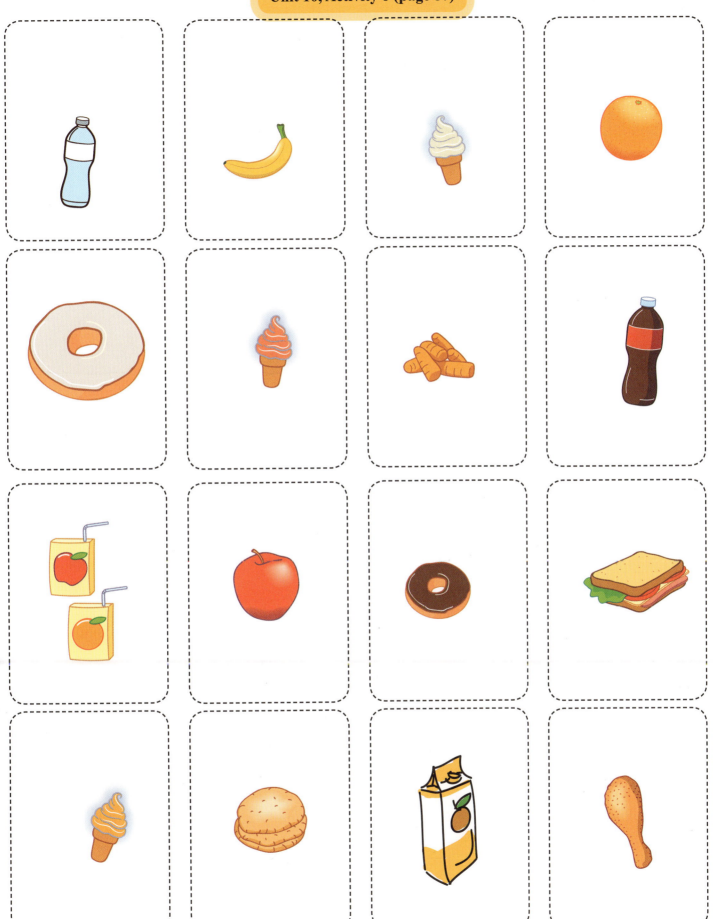

Unit 12, Activity 10 (page 107)

Partner One

**Unit 12, Activity 10 (page 107)**

**Partner Two**

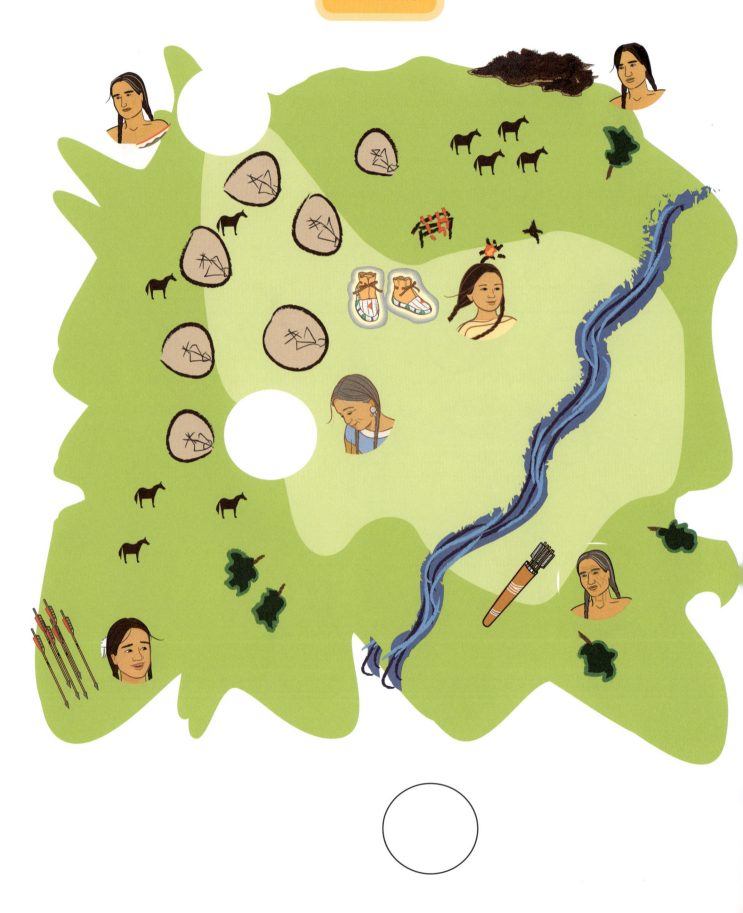

Unit 12, Activity 5 (page 105)

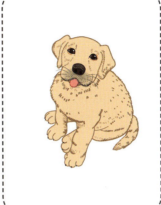

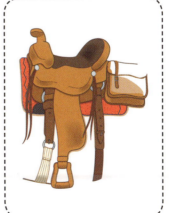